Dropping Gemz
365
for her

Advance praise for *Dropping Gemz 365 for her*

Dropping Gemz 365 is a self-help book comprised of a compilation of motivational thoughts and virtues that will help you take control of your thoughts and encourage you to think positively, propelling you forward. Each thought is represented as a Gem, and you'll gain a Gem every day of the year. The Gemz that are shared each day will empower you to forgive yourself and focus your thoughts. These Gemz will help direct your energy, preparing you for positive outcomes. You'll collect your Gemz one at a time and cherish them deep in your heart as you reach your own personal enlightenment. You'll be able to use this valuable collection of Gemz by applying them to any challenge you may face!

—*Aswan F.,*
Dearborn, Michigan

Dropping Gemz

365

for her

NEJAN L. DANE

UNCOVER LIFE'S TREASURES EVERY DAY OF THE YEAR TO ILLUMINATE YOUR OWN BEST VERSION

Cover Design by FormattedBooks

Library of Congress Control Number: 2022919851

All rights reserved.

ISBNs
979-8-9861874-0-2 (print), 979-8-9861874-1-9 (hardcover)
979-8-9861874-2-6 (ebook), 979-8-9861874-3-3 (audiobook)

Printed in the United States of America

To those who love and support me every step of the way and tell me I am called to greatness. You know who you are! Love you.

—*Nejan L. Dane*

#DG365
#DroppingGemz365
"The Gemstone Way"

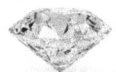

JANUARY 1 GEM
Don't share until it's done.

Gemstone, much like it's wise to not tell everybody your business, it's best not to share with others or talk too much about what you're "cooking up" or what goals you're setting in motion until well—you've completed them.

In psychology, the act of disclosing or oversharing huge goals is equivalent to generating the same feelings and emotions you experience when you actually accomplish those goals. The false sense of satisfaction that comes from the praise and acknowledgment of others for merely working towards your goals creates a false narrative that can make you feel like you've achieved your goal already.

This inadvertently results in a greater chance of you not following through with your actual goals because of the artificial feeling of completion that accommodates premature recognition and celebration.

So, keep quiet, keep at it, and *don't share until it's done.*

JANUARY 2 GEM
Ask for 100%.

"Shoot for the moon! You may land in the stars." This saying applies to asking for what you want.

Don't downgrade whatever you are asking for, Gemstone. Ask for exactly what you want, because what you want is what you want...and that's what you want.

You have greater potential for receiving a greater percentage of what you want (maybe even 100%!) just by asking for it. "Go for the jugular," as the phrase goes, and *ask for 100%*. After all, you won't be disappointed if you land with ninety-nine.

JANUARY 3 GEM
Invest in yourself.

Simply put, whatever you're good at, put your time, money, and energy into that. Feed your talents, Gemstone.

Your natural talents are a gift from above (Rom. 12:6—8). Operating within your God-given talents allows you to excel and also helps you help others (Prov. 18:16). Many people have trouble realizing what their gift is because it comes so naturally to them. It's hard for them to accept that their gift is a gift, but others always see it.

If you struggle with figuring out what your gift is, think about times when people have said to you, "Wow, you're really good at that!" What were you doing then? Think about what you know how to do that's pretty easy for you but is challenging for others. Is it singing, public speaking, or caregiving? Or maybe leading, baking, doing interior design, teaching, or developing a business? Maybe it's hairstyling.

Whatever comes naturally to you only requires some refining, whereas the things that don't come easily require a great deal of learning, studying, imitating, and replicating.

Invest in yourself. Invest in your natural, God-given talents to grow and expand your talents and to get a maximum return on your investments.

JANUARY 4 GEM
A power move.

Often, you may find yourself being a friend's "brain" or the "brain" of a professional group or team. Now it's time to flip the switch! For once, scale back on being the head of the pack, the know-it-all, the go-to person, the head honcho, the numero uno, the nucleus, the "brain."

Don't let this piece of advice scare you. This is certainly not about stripping away any of your power—it's a *power move*, Gemstone. Take a step back and learn from others. Value their opinions and input.

How can you ever gain new knowledge and grow if you're always the leader of the pack? Where's the reciprocity of "each one teach one" in that?

That said, if you've completely outgrown a group, while it doesn't hurt to stay connected to them, you need to find more people of greater intelligence to surround yourself with.

There is no reason to stunt your personal or your professional growth, not ever!

JANUARY 5 GEM
Take something off your plate.

Constantly creating is the only way to keep growing your business and your brand.

Amazon's former CEO Jeff Bezos (a.k.a. "Billionaire Bezos") stepped down from being Amazon's CEO in 2021. The billionaire got out of the day-to-day operations of the business in order to dedicate more of his time to inventing.

Gemstone, what role can you *take off your plate* so that you can pay more attention to the inventions spinning in your wheelhouse, the things you really want to further explore, and make come to fruition?

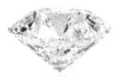

JANUARY 6 GEM
Become debt-free.

What are you willing to sacrifice to *become debt-free?* It's really the little things that add up to create debt: the multiple streaming apps, the name-brand stuff, the constant eating and going out, and more.

Gemstone, again, the question is, what are you willing to sacrifice for a few months (or a year or two) to financially get to where you want and need to be?

List five things you're willing to cut back on. C'mon, where's your willpower? You have it buried in there somewhere to commit yourself to *becoming debt-free!*

Use the extra funds to pay down the principal balance attached to your lowest debt. Go over and above that regular monthly payment! Paying extra on the principal balance can significantly reduce the amount of interest you'll pay for the life of that debt.

Focus on paying off one debt at a time while still making regular monthly payments on all the others. Also consider debt consolidation to lower your total monthly payments and improve your cash flow.

Use online financial calculators to see how making additional payments on the principal can help you save a lot of money over time. Explore opportunities to consolidate your personal debt with private investors (i.e., regular people) who are willing to take on more risks by financing your debt via crowdfunding versus consolidating debt with a financial institution (where debt consolidation qualifications may be more stringent).

Download free credit monitoring apps to keep track of your credit score and credit report. Such apps will also send you daily tips customized to your situation. Then use those tips to improve your financial position!

JANUARY 7 GEM
Make a 180° turn.

Take one full day to cry, moan, and complain. After your boo-hoo and woe-is-me session, it's time to do what soldiers are commanded to do in the military: an "about-face"! That's right—*make a 180° turn* to change the direction you're facing. Reverse your course.

Do not make a 360° move that takes you right back to where you were before you started doing a full twirl! *Doing a 180° turn* means making a transformation; it means ending up in a place where things are completely different than they were before. Don't confuse the two! To *make a 180° turn* in life means you're changing the way you think and the way you make decisions but making a 360° turn is doing nothing but rotating in a full circle and winding up in the same old patterns of thinking and doing. Oh, what a vicious cycle that can be!

Gemstone, it's time to put your big-girl panties on. Stop sulking! Put a new plan in motion. Get therapy and help when you need it, of course, but toughen the heck up! You are not weak and this little upset or setback will not take you out.

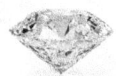

JANUARY 8 GEM
Trust character.

After a while, you can become a great judge of character. People tend to ditch their "representative" fronts much more quickly these days, especially after they've gotten what they really wanted.

Once you've broken down their fourth wall—the whole "show" they're putting on—who they really are appears. Surprise! She's really a hater, an op, a mean girl. Surprise! He's really a liar, a player, a user.

Gemstone, *trust the character* behind the fourth wall. It always surfaces. When it does, don't ignore it! Treat it the way you should and give nothing more when you know nothing more should be given. Close the curtains on them—the show's over!

JANUARY 9 GEM
Irrational decisions are made amid chaos.

Gemstone, are you being tapped to make a decision in the heat of the moment? Are people pressuring you to buy or invest in something costly without giving you time to logically think about why you should buy it?

You need at least 24 to 72 hours to research and leverage objective and historical data, think things through logically, and analyze what's being put in front of you before you can make a sound decision. You can't let yourself be forced into suddenly making a decision.

If someone asks you for a fast decision, if you're somewhat interested, your response should be "Not right now—I need more time to think about it." If you know right away that you're completely uninterested, then your response should be a hard "No."

Your decision is more likely to be an irrational one if you're feeling forced to make it when in reality you need to think about the situation at length. Clarity and not chaos is what you need to determine if you should proceed.

Always process your decision away from the person who's persistently asking you to decide.

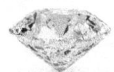

JANUARY 10 GEM
You lose it if you don't use it.

What a waste—you learned all of that and didn't even use it! If you invest your time in learning something and then you never apply it, consider it a distant memory.

In Psychology 101, you learn about memory muscles. Those memory muscles help resharpen stale skills. Revisit your buried talents and skills, Gemstone! Start putting them back into use.

Work that memory muscle and bring your brain back to life!

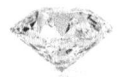

JANUARY 11 GEM
Have fun!

All work and no play? Gemstone, be sure to designate time to just *have fun*! Choose a day out of the week to do something you enjoy during your leisure hours.

Having fun is necessary. It helps break up the monotony of going to work, paying bills, pumping gas, picking up the kids, and doing every other robotic thing you do when your feet hit the ground each morning.

Not only is *having fun* good for the heart and soul, it's also good for your mental health. It's a sure way to reset your mind from the everyday challenges you deal with.

Now, go *have fun*!

JANUARY 12 GEM

Get therapy.

Hold hands and say it together: "Ahh...therapy." It's the new thing!

Get with the program and *get a therapist*, stat! These days and times, everyone needs one.

Many health insurance providers are connecting their plan participants to live therapists who are virtually available 24/7 and are covered in your health plan. Check your specific plan for this new coverage.

Licensed professionals can help you navigate through sore spots from your childhood as well as recent and past traumas to help you understand "you" better and give you strategies for living your best life. Getting support for mental health needs is no longer stigmatized.

Gemstone, the wellness of your mind is just as important as the wellness of your physical body.

No shame. No game. *Get therapy.*

JANUARY 13 GEM
The successful versus the unsuccessful.

"Successful people do daily what only
unsuccessful people do occasionally."
—John C. Maxwell.

The work you put in every day serves a purpose.

Your dedication is the backbone of your success.

Meanwhile, the occasional doer will experience irregular results consistently.

Again, the occasional doer will experience irregular results consistently—guaranteed.

Gemstone, be consistent to be successful.

JANUARY 14 GEM
Categorize your friends.

Gemstone, you are responsible for defining exactly who your friends are and what they mean to you. Classifying your friends by the type of relationship you have with them is wise.

This method allows you to understand what purpose each of your friends serves. In doing so, you are putting your friendships into proper perspective. That means you'll hold a "shopping buddy" blameless for their lack of emotional support when you're going through a bad breakup.

Putting the wrong expectations on friends is unfair to them and is something that has unnecessarily ended friendships. That's because friends cannot ever live up to a wrongful categorization of them. Your "emotional support" friend may not be your "problem-solver" friend, and it's up to you to know the difference. Friendship categories are endless and up to your discretion.

Categorize your friends by naming them as confidantes, travel pals, retail therapy crew, problem-solvers, jail-bailers, the have-fun-and-keep-it-light group, the prayer warriors and encouragers, and any other friendship categories you deem necessary. Some friends can fit into more than one category. If you have a friend who fits into all categories, consider yourself blessed! That's indeed a lifetime friend.

JANUARY 15 GEM
Avoid batshit crazy people.

According to the Urban Dictionary, *"batshit crazy"* is a term used to identify a person who is certifiably nuts, while the Merriam-Webster Dictionary refers to the phrase as being a vulgar slang term that views a person as irrational, excited, and angry, a.k.a. CRAZY.

Gemstone, the following piece of advice is worth millions of dollars, so don't forget it:

Avoid batshit crazy people at all costs to preserve your sanity.

JANUARY 16 GEM
Disengage from the conversation.

Gemstone, don't allow people to talk to you crazy—make them respect you.

Inform people immediately that you will not tolerate disrespect and that they cannot talk to you in just any kind of way. This clearly creates boundaries as to how people should address you in conversation.

Tell violators that you are *disengaging from the conversation* with them and do not give them a second warning if they continue. Fully turn your back on them and walk away or hang up the phone. Firmly disengaging lets them know that you are serious. And do not reach back out to them. This reinforces that you mean what you say. If you are not interested in severing the relationship, just stop and leave it be.

Take a breather and allow them to reach back out to you respectfully after some time has gone by. If the offense was great, avoid responding to text message apologies from them—that's a poor substitute for them giving you the proper apology you deserve.

Receive their proper apology and reiterate the reason why you *disengaged from the conversation* with them. Also clearly state the acceptable way to communicate with you going forward.

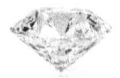

JANUARY 17 GEM
What's the difference?

While you're sitting down, they're over there getting it done. That's the difference.

There are too many resources and too much free information and guidance out in the world for you to be over there complaining about what you can't do.

Gemstone, it's time to hang up your excuses—they're old, tired, and washed up. Enough already. Just do it! And if you can't do it, do it anyway!

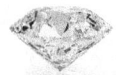

JANUARY 18 GEM
Your opinion is yours.

You have the right to change your mind. You can like something today and hate it tomorrow. The right to switch *your opinion is yours.*

After having gained new information or after having heard both sides of an issue and given the matter much thought, changing your viewpoint is absolutely acceptable. Do not allow others to tell you otherwise.

Stop believing you must be 100% committed to your original viewpoint just because you're afraid that others will see you differently if you change your mind.

Changing your opinion about something when you want to, Gemstone, is about being true to your inner thoughts and beliefs.

Now, say: "Alexa, play 'True to Myself' by Ziggy Marley."

JANUARY 19 GEM
Extend grace.

Simply put, grace is unmerited favor that is given from above and then adapted by humanity. It is synonymous with mercy and kindness.

Think back to the most recent time you received grace. Did a friend give you a pass for being late to dinner? Did you forget to fulfill a promise but the person didn't get mad, or were you given more time to complete an assignment or a project past the deadline without any repercussions? Did you make a huge mistake but didn't have to suffer the consequences because you were forgiven? That's grace.

Do you remember how good it made you feel to receive such undeserved favor, Gemstone? You heaved a sigh of relief, right? When you were met with grace, you may have even experienced released endorphins that brought your stress and anxiety levels all the way back down.

Now think again: when was the last time you *extended grace* to someone? Was it yesterday, last week, a month ago? Find a reason to *extend grace* today.

Giving grace is "being there" for someone. It's matching their emotions by being happy when they're happy, mourning with them when they mourn, and "letting it go" by keeping a peaceful spirit when they are less than kind.

Life is hard enough! Everyone needs a little grace, so extend it.

JANUARY 20 GEM
Know what you don't know.

If you're seemingly part of a conversation but you hear a word, phrase, expression, or topic being discussed that's unfamiliar to you, don't ignore that unknown idea. Figure out what the heck you don't know so that you can keep your mind sharp. Google it right away!

Gemstone, don't wait for others to explain what something means. That's nonproductive. Keep your mind in a state of growing! Remember, the opposite of growing is shrinking, diminishing, decreasing, failing. Essentially, not growing equals dying.

So *know what you don't know* to grow...and grow, grow, grow...and know, know, know.

JANUARY 21 GEM
Stop telling your business.

Everyone does not need to know all your business! That includes people who are close to you.

People are entitled to have their opinions about you but stop giving them reasons to have one.

Gemstone, not everything is always meant to be shared. So, hush.

JANUARY 22 GEM

Don't stay in the middle.

Pick a side. Pick a side. Stop toying with where you stand on things!

Gemstone, let your "yes" be "yes" and your "no" be "no." Stop being so miserably lukewarm. Aren't you tired of being in the middle of how you feel?

Your morals, values, and goals should help keep you aligned by leading the decisions you make in life. Be clear about what you want and what you don't want. Deep down, you feel a certain way for a reason, and it's time to settle on that reason. That's what makes you *you*.

If you are finding yourself to be frequently indecisive and on the fence about your life choices, then you need to gain more clarity. Reassess your morals, values, and goals to help you take a stance.

JANUARY 23 GEM
Find the mole.

Got a leak in your camp of girlfriends, in the workplace, or even in your family?

Gemstone, *find the mole* by making up a story (or think of a real one you don't care about) and then sharing it separately with those you think might be the mole. Change a specific detail in the story when you tell each person. That way, when the story gets out, you will find the mole based on the version of the story that's out there.

There, it's settled! You know who your mole is. Now let that be the last time you tell them your business.

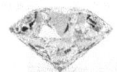

JANUARY 24 GEM
Become culturally acquainted.

So you want to expand your horizons but have yet to tap into an environment beyond your own? Hmmm… That's giving you are very "unseasoned" culturally.

Whether you're in a financial position to travel or not, it's time to get started on the basics of becoming more culturalized! Begin your journey through the seven continents: gain an understanding of who other people are, how they live, and how their society contributes to the world.

Gemstone, tap into different cultures by engaging with locals when you're out of the country. If it's safe, do more than just excursions offered to you by the resort. Go beyond touristy hot spots and converse with locals about their way of life, their country's government and politics, their cost of living, their traditions and rituals, and what matters most to them.

You can't take over the world without knowing about it, so become more culturally rounded to *become culturally acquainted.* Test your global mindset for free by taking the Global Attitude Protocol (GAP) survey at ghemawat.com/surveys.

JANUARY 25 GEM
Stop over apologizing.

After you've said your apology once with real intent, there's no need to keep at it. It just becomes a broken record.

And not everything requires an apology—you might just need to explain the situation and that's about it.

Always look for solutions for moving forward, Gemstone. Over apologizing is only reliving whatever you apologized for the first time.

JANUARY 26 GEM

Break through your breaking point.

Gemstone, when you are on the verge of giving up is typically when you're very close to breaking through.

Your breaking point is only a hurdle coming from within. When you push through and jump over that hurdle, then you've elevated yourself to the next level. If the mind believes it is capable of doing something, it has a greater chance of accomplishing it.

The power of the mind is incredible! As part of the nervous system, what you're thinking is transmitted throughout your body, producing and releasing hormones that make up your emotional state.

Breaking through something is mentally taking the limits off whatever is holding you back, and this process starts with your greatest muscle: your brain.

You absolutely have to believe that you can do it in order to *break through your breaking point.*

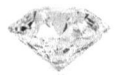

JANUARY 27 GEM
The blue pill versus the red pill.

Are you ready to take the red pill and
"see how deep the rabbit hole goes?"
—Morpheus

In the 1999 film *The Matrix*, Morpheus (played by Laurence Fishburne) gives Neo (played by Keanu Reeves) the option to continue being naïve and socially pro-grammed by taking the blue pill or face harsh-yet-true, stark reality by taking the red pill.

When you were a child, you were given the blue pill by your parents to shield you from a mean, cold, scary world and to keep you from the painstaking and vile truths that can steal a young child's innocence and bliss. But today, you are no stranger to the red pill. You see things, people, and the world for what they really are. You have an un-sugar-coated, raw, savage outlook.

However, do not permanently dispose of the blue pill just yet! Many people are choosing to take both the blue pill and the red pill and letting those realities coexist. This could be your blended reality, too.

Gemstone, can you accept your life being a healthy mixture of both pills? Could you potentially take a purple pill? The combination of both will give you a more bal-anced take on life. You will care less about what others think of you, you'll have a higher level of consciousness regarding life decisions, and you will be more in tune with your motivations and the positive influences in your life.

So, what color view on life would you like? The red one, the blue one, or the purple one? Your choice.

JANUARY 28 GEM
Think ahead.

Abandon short-term thinking by *thinking ahead.*

Start thinking about how you can make calculated moves today that will positively impact you in 5 to 10 years, putting you ahead of the game.

Seasoned creators, inventors, and serious investors always think long-term. Consider your true north, Gemstone, by knowing your endgame.

How can the moves you make today put you one step closer to achieving some of your biggest and wildest dreams?

JANUARY 29 GEM
"You've changed," they say.

Were you not supposed to change? Gemstone, if you're not changing, then what are you doing?

When people criticize you for not being who you used to be—or when they bring up your past mistakes, mishaps, and failures and those no longer resonate with you—then you've realized your elevation.

You have grown beyond who they've known you to be and how they've always seen you. You've removed the transparency around yourself. You have reinvented yourself and recreated yourself anew.

This is growth!

Embrace the *"You've changed"* type of criticism. It's a key indicator that you have evolved and that your evolution is noticeable.

Reconsider those acquaintances who are still stuck on who you were yesterday and not who you are today.

JANUARY 30 GEM
"No one asked."

Gemstone, saying *"No one asked"* is a genius response to give when people realize later that you had the answer they needed all along.

They discounted your intelligence from the beginning and never asked for your advice. Therefore, they had to go through things the hard way.

What a valuable lesson people will never forget when they didn't ask the expert...namely, you!

JANUARY 31 GEM
Your daily affirmations.

Gemstone, approach each day with positivity by refocusing your mindset, suspending disbelief, and believing in yourself.

Recite these 20 affirmations daily:

1. I am wise and make smart decisions.
2. I am beautiful, kind, loving, and gracious, and all who know me vividly see these characteristics within me.
3. I am intelligent and stand out professionally at every meeting table and in every room.
4. I am the epitome of self-control and I protect my aura from self-destruction.
5. I am making choices today that will positively impact my future.
6. My age does not play a factor in my ability to accomplish anything I desire in life.
7. I fully execute my talents and gifts at 100% with none gone to waste.
8. I am my ideal weight and I maintain my weight through healthy eating, exercising, cleansing, and pursuing a disciplined and balanced lifestyle.
9. I immediately block negativity out of my life and refuse to allow others to control my narrative.

10. I am not afraid of my past or what people will do or say about me, because they have no power over me.

11. I forgive myself for my mistakes and for having taken purposeful actions that were not right and not aligned with my destiny.

12. I love myself for who I am today, for who I am tomorrow, and for who I will be in the future.

13. I am fulfilled in life, and I make time to frequently enjoy my hobbies and live out my dreams without self-judgment or guilt.

14. I grow and learn every day and have a broad range of perspectives.

15. I am creative and I attract and generate wealth.

16. I turn every lesson learned into an opportunity to grow and elevate.

17. I celebrate my small wins to cultivate self-love and self-worth.

18. I was created to do amazing things in life and I will and I shall.

19. I am patient with my body when it needs rest, healing, and rejuvenation.

20. I release anything that does not serve me or my purpose and I rebuke unconstructiveness in my life.

FEBRUARY 1 GEM
Boss up!

Turn up the notch to high heat and set it ablaze, because the time has come to *boss up* by taking full control of your life!

How?

Direct all of your time, energy, and resources to your main goals in life. Shift your gear into overdrive and accelerate full speed ahead with your pedal to the metal to perform at top level with major force.

You'll need self-esteem to get this done. How do you get that?

Straighten your crown, Gemstone, adjust your sash, and place your desk nameplate front and center. Roll up your sleeves and be intentional with what you need to get done. No more time for games and only imagining! It's time to take some serious action and leave procrastination in the past.

Boss up! As Alicia Keys says, be the girl who's "on fire."

FEBRUARY 2 GEM
Keep it to yourself.

Keep your complaints to yourself today.

Go through the entire day without whining, because honestly, nobody wants to hear it.

Again, no one—literally no one—wants to hear it. They don't need your negativity disturbing their chakras.

Your constant complaining is quite aggravating, and it needs to stop.

Thank you kindly, Gemstone.

FEBRUARY 3 GEM

You hear it and you see it.

Life sends soft and subtle hints when things have the potential to become problematic.

Gemstone, you must not turn a blind eye to these warning signals. As Oprah Winfrey says, "Life whispers to you all the time."

Life is endlessly sending you messages. Life's inklings are not to be ignored! When you ignore the forewarnings of life's potential disasters, the situation will have then positioned itself to control you and overpower you.

Yes, *you hear it and you see it.* Don't disregard or overlook those faint rumblings! Face your issues to prevent them from becoming unmanageable.

Respond to life's cues to counter any intimidation of your livelihood, to avert bad outcomes, and to prevent crises.

FEBRUARY 4 GEM
Practice self-love.

You must love yourself before you can truly love and care for others.

Self-love has nothing to do with being selfish—rather, it has everything to do with putting yourself first. It is having a strong admiration for your own well-being and contentment by ensuring that your needs are being met and that you're not sacrificing your welfare to please others.

Self-love is synonymous with what flight attendants communicate on every flight, which is to put your own oxygen mask on first before aiding anyone else in case of an emergency. This is so that you won't run out of oxygen and die while trying to help others.

The same concept applies to *self-love*: put your health and wellness first, Gemstone, so that you can live and be available to others in the right kind of way.

FEBRUARY 5 GEM
Show up 80%.

In a study conducted on free enterprise, entrepreneurs shared that showing up accounts for most of their success, while the other 20% speaks to their grind, intellect, and follow-up skills.

If 80% of success is accounted for by just showing up, what more motivation do you need to roll out of the bed, shower, put on some clean drawers and clothes, fix your face, get on your good foot, and go?

Gemstone, it's so easy to give 80%. Don't make this hard.

Show up today!

FEBRUARY 6 GEM
Embrace slow living.

The state of serenity is being calm, peaceful, and untroubled.

How can one experience such a tranquil inner climate? It starts with creating a therapeutic routine.

The YouTube channel *Malama Life* provides "slow living" and minimalistic content for helping you set the stage for pure relaxation. This captivating channel embraces the slow movement lifestyle that originated in Bra, Italy in the late 1980s, expanding from the concept of organic foods to the state of meaningful connectedness.

Regulate your stress levels by being intentional about slowing down the fast pace of life whenever you need to, Gemstone.

There are many ways to regulate your stress levels: meditating, journaling, enjoying sleep sounds from your Alexa or Google device, practicing yoga, doing breathwork, embracing mindfulness, or listening to soft, mellow music playing amid dim lighting to help you connect with your inner thoughts.

Late at night or in the wee hours of the morning when all is quiet and your home is at rest is when you may be able to encapsulate serenity. Challenge yourself daily to experience moments of tranquility. This is time for you to reset. You will not regret the time you spend in serenity.

FEBRUARY 7 GEM
Make a bucket list.

Make your bucket list—life is made to be lived!

Make a list of some of the most fun and outlandish things you want to do in life and share your list with others. Sharing your bucket list is also a great and fun way for people to get to know you better.

Gemstone, open up about who you are and your versatility. Your bucket list should consist of 25 random things you want to do. List your grandest ideas.

Writing down your bucket list gives life to your "inner you," but doing what's on your bucket list is you living your life to the fullest.

Live your life!

FEBRUARY 8 GEM
Brand yourself.

Branding yourself means uniquely setting yourself apart professionally and within your social circles through consistent and coherent messaging. You'll strategically present this messaging in person and online through an effective social media strategy.

At its core, *branding yourself* is encouraging people to invest in you! Carefully crafted, your brand should communicate your identity, values, differentiation, experience, and position so that your audience can better understand who you are.

In business school, students are tasked with analyzing huge company brands in order to understand the essence of who and what the brands are and the impact they have on consumers in terms of driving sales and customer loyalty.

Gemstone, take the time today to think about your own personal brand. Is it clear? Is it consistent? Does your individual brand fully speak to who you are and the value you bring to the table?

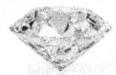

FEBRUARY 9 GEM
It's not lonely at the top.

Are you afraid to go all the way to the top because you've heard it's lonely up there? What a very untrue belief that is! The journey to get there may feel lonely, but being at the top is not lonely.

It's not lonely at the top—you just don't know the people up there. Yet.

Being at the top only feels lonely because you're unfamiliar with those who are already up there. Gemstone, they are waiting for you to join them!

FEBRUARY 10 GEM
Get it done.

Stop procrastinating about what you know you need to get done and just do it.

The primary reason most people keep putting something off is because they don't feel like doing it.

Whatever needs to get done requires time, brainpower, and/or physical energy, and it just doesn't seem like a priority—even though it is. If you're honest with yourself, what needs to get done is not getting done because you're lazy or you have a fear of failure or you're unmotivated or you need help or...the list goes on and on.

Gemstone, acknowledge the real reason you are not *getting it done* and own that reason. Write out what the outcomes will be if you complete your lingering task as well as what the consequences will be if you don't. Then settle on accomplishing the task by incentivizing yourself for *getting it done* by setting and meeting your deadline.

Incentives for accomplishing your unique task could be many: a new outfit, an exquisite meal, a spa day, a day trip, a new purse, your favorite ice cream or dessert, a night out with friends.

Get it done.

FEBRUARY 11 GEM
Be on time.

Gemstone, make a concerted effort to *be on time*. Being late or fashionably late is not cute.

Habitually late people earn their negative label. It's rude to be late to places, activities, and events, especially when other people's money and time are involved. Tardiness is very disrespectful.

People get tired of this behavior after a while and will just stop inviting you out. There's no need for them to continue to wait on someone who doesn't value their time. That said, people will be understanding of competing priorities and they will understand that things happen.

Stop taking advantage of people's grace for your chronic lateness. Be intentional with *being on time*. Be respectful of others' time. If you don't want to attend an event, tell them so.

FEBRUARY 12 GEM
Know what's understood.

Where there's the meeting of the minds and synergies, there's no need to state the obvious, because Gemstone, what's understood does not have to be explained.

Save your breath.

FEBRUARY 13 GEM
Gain wisdom.

Having wisdom is having a level of intelligence and discernment.

Wisdom is usually obtained through knowledge, experience, reading, and learning from others. Not everyone possesses wisdom—after all, we see people make stupid decisions repeatedly and daily.

Gemstone, you do not have to be old to be wise. Through continuous learning, reading, observing, studying what remarkable people do and say, listening more, and communicating from a place of knowledge and intelligence, you will increase your wisdom.

FEBRUARY 14 GEM
End bad soul ties.

Your soul is composed of your mind, will, emotions, and the "ties" that link you to others. Soul ties are the spiritual and emotional connections between two souls.

This "knitting together" of two souls is formed in many ways, but these three ways stand out: forming close relationships, making verbal promises to each other, and sharing sexual intimacy.

Soul ties are good except when they are bad. Good soul ties are when two people operate in unison, evenly yoked and spiritually aligned. Bad soul ties are when one person or both people are confused about the relationship and feel miserable, drained, manipulated, or abused by the other person. Bad soul ties can be extremely difficult to break because of the love one person has for the other and (mostly) because of the amount of time that's been invested in the relationship.

Walking away from the many years you've spent connected to a person will feel like a significant loss. It's similar to the feelings you'd get at that person's funeral because of the intrinsic value of the time you spent with them and your deep love for them.

4 ways to end bad soul ties:

- ✓ Praying and asking God to help you break the soul tie.
- ✓ Forgiving the other person and yourself and releasing yourself from the relationship.
- ✓ Cutting off all lines of communication with the person.
- ✓ Ridding yourself of all material things that connect you to them.

Gemstone, for deeper healing, consider religious cognitive–emotional therapy (RCET) for greater assistance with breaking bad soul ties.

FEBRUARY 15 GEM
Encourage others.

"Everybody needs somebody sometimes."

Gemstone, this saying rings true now more than ever.

You are not the only one going through something—everyone has their fair share of battles to fight and hills to climb. That's part of life.

Encourage others more often. When you do, subconsciously, you are also encouraging yourself and shifting your own mindset for the better.

FEBRUARY 16 GEM
Stop the drama.

For God's sake, please stop! Give up the antics already. Stop being entangled in drama all the time.

Aren't you tired of seeking attention this way? Because that's exactly what you're doing.

Calm your wild, loud, uncontrollable, and outbursting self and notch things all the way down. Hang up the adult temper tantrums, take "several seats," and mellow out.

Gemstone, learn to use your words intelligently and respectfully to communicate your concerns.

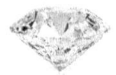

FEBRUARY 17 GEM
Pursue mental fitness.

Exercising is a physical habit you need to create to ensure that you're maximizing your health. Along with a healthy diet, exercise also helps increase your lifespan.

Doing physical fitness 3 to 5 times a week is good for keeping your heart rate up, your blood circulating, and oxygen pumping to your organs.

But Gemstone, there's another component to fitness beyond moving around your physical body, and that is exercising your brain.

Exercising your brain—also known as *pursuing mental fitness*—increases its vitality and improves its neuroplasticity, which is part of what enables us to store and access memories.

According to *Forbes,* in its May 2021 article, "Fitness Isn't Just Physical: The Importance of Exercising," you can exercise your brain by doing active reading, piecing together puzzles, practicing mindfulness, traveling, listening to music, and more. In a nutshell, you can modify your neural connections to rewire your brain and enhance your quality of life.

FEBRUARY 18 GEM
Cut them off.

Gemstone, the shifty behaviors you see in others are signs. Your intuition is not lying to you!

If you're not "feeling" that something is right, then you know what time it is: it's time to "peace out."

Investigate the situation and then separate yourself from it. Remove yourself quickly from those you know you need to cut off. You know exactly who they are.

Allow reading this today to serve as another con-firmation that *cutting them off* from your life needs to happen.

Chop-chop!

FEBRUARY 19 GEM
Isolation.

In the quietest moments away from all the noise and external forces, you'll find yourself alone.

Being alone can feel lonely at times, but it's good for you and good for your soul. You become unexposed to the pressures and judgments that others may impose. During isolation, you can think, reminisce, dream, and process.

Gemstone, your isolation will be an awakening to self-discovery:

I — Imagination expands
S — Solidarity is activated
O — Opportunities are revealed
L — Layers are removed
A — Art is formed
T — The third eye awakens
I — Ideas flow
O — Opposition is neutralized
N — Nostalgia transpires

FEBRUARY 20 GEM
Shift your method.

So you haven't learned yet? You just keep doing the same thing over and over to no avail.

You keep getting the same results, which are nothing but disappointments and heartaches. This behavior is asinine! Your results have literally not changed because you have not changed your method or approach. This is insanity.

What you are continually doing is not working—it is not solving your problem. Your hypothesis has been tested repeatedly and without a doubt has failed.

So what now?

Gemstone, it's time to deviate. *Shift your method* or approach. Identify what needs to change in the process of whatever you are trying to accomplish. Sometimes, only a minor change may be required; other times, a more significant change is necessary.

Rework the process until you achieve your desired results.

FEBRUARY 21 GEM
Stop faking it.

If you don't like something, then Gemstone, you just don't!

Stop pretending that you like something just to appease others—that gets very tiring.

Stop operating inauthentically. Everyone is different; therefore, differences of opinion should always be welcomed.

Be honest about how someone or something makes you feel. Be clear on what you like and be clear on what you don't like.

Preference is preference, so ditch the fakeness.

FEBRUARY 22 GEM
Choose truth.

People tell lies every day to avoid the consequences that may be associated with telling the truth.

Now more than ever, integrity has gone out the window.

Lying is an unnecessary evil that discredits and erodes character. It takes more guts to tell the truth than it takes to tell a lie.

When a person lies, they must keep up their falsities to maintain their lie. Whew! That's a lot of work!

But here's the thing: sooner or later, people will piece together when someone is a liar.

Steer clear from liars, Gemstone, because the truth is not in them.

Always *choose truth.*

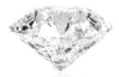

FEBRUARY 23 GEM
Nodding your head.

In communication, *nodding your head* signals that you agree with or understand what is being shared.

Actively listen in conversations and limit nodding your head—even if you agree with what the person is saying. Gemstone, give yourself time to process what is being communicated versus *nodding your head* up and down throughout the conversation.

It's human nature for others to believe that your head nods mean you understand and agree with the information being shared, taught, or explained.

To improve your communication skills, instead of nodding, verbalize your agreement and summarize your understanding of what the other person said and why you agree with them.

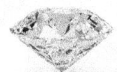

FEBRUARY 24 GEM
Passive income.

Gemstone, *"passive income"* is a very popular term these days. Acquiring *passive income* is an earner's dream since it (often) requires minimal labor to make and maintain it.

There are many ways to start making *passive income*, like renting properties, flipping retail products, gaining dividends on stock, blogging/vlogging, creating apps, creating online courses, and writing e-books. The list is endless.

However, the very best and easiest way to generate *passive income* is by flexing your own talents and gifts. Your talents and gifts are the things that come naturally to you; you were born with them.

If you struggle with knowing what your inherent skills are, think of what people commend you on all the time—the things you're really good at without even trying. Your family and friends know what you're very good at and will tell you right away if you ask them.

Doing what comes effortlessly to you and using it to generate additional income will be the quickest way for you to start creating wealth.

FEBRUARY 25 GEM
Avoid shifty people.

Yes, they're everywhere! Shifty people are people who tend to be untransparent or divisive. You can't trust them. They tell you one thing but then do another. Trust them to be exactly who and what they are: shifty.

Gemstone, believe them the first time.

Shifty people are known to repeatedly lie, steal, deceive, cheat, not follow through on their word, and gaslight people.

Avoid shifty people!

FEBRUARY 26 GEM
Could you repeat that?

If you don't understand something, ask for clarity.

Acting as if you heard or understood someone when you really didn't is absurd. It's better to ask someone to re-explain themselves versus making assumptions and trying to piece together their words and the information they shared.

Gemstone, if you notice that you're always asking someone to repeat themselves, then that's a great opportunity for you to practice active listening. Active listening is being engaged in what's being communicated by listening 80% of the time and speaking 20% of the time.

Reflect on their viewpoint and ask follow-up questions to confirm your understanding. Save your rebuttal or perspective for when you have the floor.

FEBRUARY 27 GEM
Find something to laugh at.

Laugh, laugh, and laugh.

Find time to just laugh since laughter does the heart good like medicine, just like the ol' folks say (Prov. 17:22).

Gemstone, life is hard enough already. There's no need for you to be shriveled up and sour all day.

Laugh at your past mistakes, failures, and stupid decisions. Laugh at comedy movies, silly social media posts, your coworker's corny jokes, music lyrics that lack substance, dumb politics, your kids being funny, ridiculous ideas that you and your friends drum up, outlandish reality TV shows, and more.

Just laugh.

FEBRUARY 28 GEM
Embrace the process.

Get through it!

Many people hate going through a process because it requires more usage of their brain and their time.

But a process is a solid structure that leads to sustainability. It's a developed, well-organized plan that is carried out. In business, organizations develop and follow processes to achieve their goals.

Stop being scatterbrained and doing things "fly by night"—that only produces mediocrity. Follow your outlined steps—day by day, bit by bit—to improve your personal effectiveness.

Gemstone, in the words of Nike, "Just do it!" Stick to the process to grow, embrace it to achieve your goals and to sustain yourself.

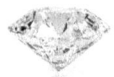

LEAP YEAR BONUS GEM
~FEBRUARY 29~
Don't be lazy.

The idea of relaxing and doing nothing all day every day sounds quite wonderful and is tempting, but it gets you nowhere.

Gemstone, you were designed to do something in life! You weren't meant to sit around and just be lazy—in other words, to be a noncontributing factor to society. Everyone has a purpose in life that needs to be carried out, and sitting around 24/7 will not help you achieve it.

It's okay to take breaks and trips and kick up your feet here and there and to rejuvenate and reenergize yourself, but the moment you decide to be permanently lazy is the moment you've changed the trajectory of what could have been an amazing and fulfilling life.

Don't be lazy!

MARCH 1 GEM
Inch it forward.

Gemstone, bit by bit, day by day, do something that gets you closer to achieving your dreams.

Everyone's daily checklist should consist of the five most important things they need to accomplish for the day, and one of those tasks needs to be something that gets you a tad closer to achieving your dreams.

It's really all the small things and minuscule tasks you perform that will help you achieve some of your greatest goals in life. Take going on a trip to the Maldives, for example. The smaller tasks involve selecting the week to go, requesting vacation time from work, booking the hotel, booking the flight, researching things to do and places to eat, and packing your suitcase. The biggest task is flying there.

But without all of the small tasks, it's hard to arrive at the big task! *Let your inches pace you forward.*

MARCH 2 GEM
Let things be.

Must you overanalyze everything and every situation? Stop trying to dig deeper for potential reasons behind every scenario.

Take things for face value and let them be, Gemstone. Stop "majoring on the minors."

Overanalyzing can lead to confusion, unnecessary worst-case scenario thinking and planning, bad assumptions, impulsive behaviors, and ruining not only your day but others'.

Let things be just what they are! Not all things need to be examined under a microscope.

MARCH 3 GEM
Record it.

Your elders are loaded with family history, wisdom, secret recipes, memorable moments, world- and life-changing events, and so much more.

Now is the perfect time to capture this information so that you'll have it for years to come.

Gemstone, create a digital time capsule by interviewing family members about everything that's essential to your family history. Your digital heirloom will be passed on for generations! It will be an invaluable way to keep and cherish your family history.

Consider distributing digital copies of your recorded family history as gifts during birthdays and holidays and at family events.

MARCH 4 GEM
7 interview prep tips.

1. Use the job posting's description, responsibilities, and qualifications as a baseline for creating your practice interview questions. Begin each question with "Tell me about a time..."
2. Practice answering all mock interview questions in STAR format (Situation, Task, Action, and Result).
3. Record your practice interview and replay it over and over to memorize your responses. This will allow you to increase your confidence and work out any kinks in your delivery.
4. Always negotiate your salary. *Most employers have a hiring salary range or budget for each position, and they normally start their offers with the lowest figure.*
5. Apply for the position even if you only meet 60% of the qualifications. Men do this all the time! *You do not always need to meet 100% of the qualifications.*
6. Find out what the hiring manager's biggest problems in their department are before the interview and share how you can help solve them.
7. Present a high-level, 90-day action plan customized to the role and its functions. Share with

the interview panel what you plan to achieve in your first 90 days. *Ensure that your action plan connects to the organization's goals and includes team engagement, building relationships and trust, and business execution.*

Now go get that job, Gemstone!

MARCH 5 GEM
Levitating.

Metaphorically, when you're *levitating*, you're floating in the air without any support.

You are on cloud nine, in a state of bliss. Life is good and you're blessed.

Gemstone, do not allow anyone to steal your feelings of well-being and elation! Not ever.

MARCH 6 GEM
Dress for success.

Financial industry expert, LAM, encourages women to not only acquire economic independence but to look like it, too, by *"dressing for success."*

Over the last decade, society has shifted more to dressing in a business-casual style to match a more casual work culture, but keep in mind that it's still worth embracing the *dress-for-success* concept to maximize your business look and set yourself apart.

The *"dress for success"* mantra still carries weight in a lot of corporate sectors. It's natural human behavior for people to take you more seriously when you dress in a professional manner.

Gemstone, observe today's top female CEOs to get a sense of executive leadership dress style. Also use Google or Siri to research some of today's best workstyles and to stay on top of fashion trends for professionals.

MARCH 7 GEM
Block toxicity.

Gemstone, *block toxicity* out of your life and quickly! If anyone adds negativity to your life or is a continual destructive disturbance, it's time to say "Byeeeee!"

Toxic people leave you emotionally drained after an encounter with them. They use intimidation as a tactic to get you to do what they want you to do, benefiting them only and ultimately making you feel highly uncomfortable. They use guilt trips to control you, which is another form of emotional bullying.

They act in a jealous way by creating invalid boundaries to keep you wrapped around their finger. They love to play the victim; they are 100% not at fault, not ever! It's always someone else's fault, and that "someone else" is you.

They put a negative spin on any compliments they may give, making them what's known as "backhanded compliments." Those are just another way to belittle, degrade, and dehumanize you and others. Toxic people are extremely defensive.

People close to them are the tail end of their jokes. When you confront toxic people about their actions, suddenly they are now the victim and are being "attacked."

How pathetic of them! *Block toxic* people.

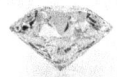

MARCH 8 GEM

Give.

Give as much as you can. It's one of the most fulfilling things you can humanly do.

Gemstone, be a good Samaritan and *give* your time, *give* your attention, *give* your love, *give* your unwanted clothes, *give* food, *give* life's necessities, and *give* wisdom, because someone is on the other side and is in need of your giving.

MARCH 9 GEM
Smile! It confuses people.

Do you know the power of your smile? When you enter a tense room, your smile alone will direct all eyes to you. Your smile will be the very first thing the crowd notices about you.

People are naturally curious and will want to know what's got your cheekbones lifted and your dimples sunken deep into your face. They'll wonder, "How is she able to smile when all hell is breaking loose and problems need to be solved and there's so much hate and decisiveness in the world?"

Your smile confuses people who aren't smiling, because they will suspect you may have a different perspective. You may have the answers they need. You may even be up to something.

Gemstone, indeed you're up to something! You're up to releasing endorphins, relieving stress, increasing your endurance, easing your pain, boosting your mood, becoming more likable and attractive, relieving your anxiety, and living longer. All of that is according to science-backed research published by the Mindfulness Meditation Institute.

Smiling is contagious! Many people will match your smile when you greet them with one.

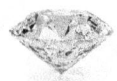

MARCH 10 GEM
Chill.

Why are you putting "twenty on ten"? Why are you hosing gasoline onto an already-lit flame? It's not even that serious...but you're making it out to be.

Seriously, *chill* and relax. Sit your attention-seeking, problematic self all the way down. Leave the dramatics for the soaps, reality TV, and toddlers going through their terrible twos.

You can easily get your point across without all the extra-ness. A firm, controlled, and respectful response speaks volumes.

Let's not be a drama queen today! Instead, Gemstone, be the mature woman that you are.

MARCH 11 GEM

Let your "yes" be "yes" and your "no" be "no."

Give no lukewarm answers. Stand by the wholesome values you passionately believe in when making decisions.

Deep down, you already know if you want to go through with something or not. You know if you want to say *"yes" or "no."* If you truly don't know, then communicate that you need more time to make the decision.

Gemstone, be direct when responding to people. Either be piping hot or freezing cold with your final decision... or be prepared to be influenced or swayed to go in a direction you really may not want to go in.

Don't be wishy-washy and give mixed messages! Not only is that annoying, people will take advantage of your indecisiveness if they sense the opportunity to do so. Be confident in saying *"yes" or "no"* and don't feel the need to overexplain your reason.

MARCH 12 GEM
Invest.

Fintech (financial technology) makes things very easy for beginner investors. The level of access for new investors today is unreal and levels the playing field—there are tons of apps on the market to download to start investing right away for as little as $1.

So, what should you *invest* in, Gemstone?

Start by investing in the places you frequently buy from, because you are a returning customer who trusts that company and deserves to have some stake in it, especially since you're spending all your money there.

Think back to some of the most recent places you spent your money. Was it Amazon, Apple, Target, or Starbucks? Be sure to read up on the company's stock performance prior to investing to see if it's worth the risk. Then once you get in the game, be sure to diversify your investment portfolio.

It's wise to stick to the rule of thumb that seasoned investors follow: "Buy low, sell high."

Remember, it's best to always consult with a qualified financial advisor or professional stock trader before engaging in any type of investing.

MARCH 13 GEM
Out the gate.

Gemstone, you came swinging *out the gate.*

"Whoa, hold your horses!" you may have heard people say. You had no facts, did not seek to understand, and failed to listen.

Next time—before you wildly react and throw a fit—get the facts! Seek to understand and listen before you respond.

MARCH 14 GEM
Dig deeper.

You are too surface-level in life.

Take your shovel and *dig deep* into who and what you really are and who you are destined to be.

You're only a few inches down. Keep digging. You still have some ways to go! Keep digging. You're not quite there. Keep digging. Go where you've never been before. Keep digging. You can go further! Keep digging. You're still not there. Keep digging.

Deeper, Gemstone, *dig deeper,* because deep down is where you'll find it.

"Find what?" you might be asking.

What you're made of.

MARCH 15 GEM
"If it's meant to be, it'll be."

"You just need to ride and see where this thing goes."
—Bebe Rexha & Florida Georgia Line

Gemstone, the saying that goes *"If it's meant to be, it'll be"* is so true when it comes to how life happens.

If you're supposed to marry that person, have that job, have those friends, live in that city, and do whatever else that's important to you, then your faith, the universe, and your atmosphere will align to ensure that it—whatever it is—happens.

What is meant to be will happen and what's not won't.

MARCH 16 GEM
You are a COVERGIRL®.

The well-known cosmetics brand *COVERGIRL®* has been endorsed over the years by the likes of the famous: Drew Barrymore, Rihanna, Molly Sims, Tyra Banks, Niki Taylor, Queen Latifah, and Christie Brinkley, to name a few.

The beauty brand represents model-worthy women and girls who are featured on magazine covers and in advertisements. Truth be told, *you too are a COVERGIRL®* because you are made in the image of God (Gen. 1:26) and God makes no mistakes.

Care about yourself and fix yourself up! That increases your self-esteem. You may be at home most days—maybe you work remotely or you're a stay-at-home mom or you run your own home-based business—but do it with self-pride.

Gemstone, show up like the *COVERGIRL®* you are and do it often! Looking as beautiful as you are is the attitude and emo-booster that will spark the inner workings of you, improving the way you see yourself from the inside out.

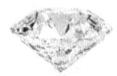

MARCH 17 GEM
Enough already!

Aren't you tired of the same old excuses? Aren't you tired of the monotony?

Aren't you tired of being broke, unhealthy, unorganized, unproductive, and unmotivated and lacking willpower? Aren't you tired of not being your own best version?

Enough already with the excuses!

Those who will, will, and those who won't, won't; those who do, do, and those who don't, don't; those who have, have, and those who have not, have not.

Take charge of your life, Gemstone, and forge ahead of your excuses.

MARCH 18 GEM
"Lights, camera, action!"

"Get up!"

"Put on your best outfit."

"Beat your face" (apply makeup).

"Practice your lines!"

"Get to location."

"Quiet on the set."

"Here's your cue."

"Action!"

"Cut...cut! Retake."

"And...scene!"

"Rehearse your lines for the next scene."

"Showtime!"

Now do it again tomorrow—and even better. The crew will roll with your best takes.

Gemstone, this is what you call showing up every day and being the best you can be, because it's your life and your show!

MARCH 19 GEM
Dominant thoughts.

Your most continually recurring thoughts will be the direction that you move in.

The power of belief is so strong that human nature moves along its path. Gemstone, whatever you're thinking about the most is what you're manifesting into reality.

Your *dominant thoughts* control your actions. Therefore, be purposeful about believing and thinking about things that are good.

Always.

MARCH 20 GEM

"Done is better than perfect."

Repeat the above declaration over and over today in your mind.

Stop trying to be perfect and just close the loop on whatever you need to get done, because perfect rarely gets done.

Even though we humans are imperfect, it is in our nature to strive for perfection. But the successful people whom you respect and admire and see living their best lives just go for it.

How?

- ✓ They start before they're ready!
- ✓ They worry about the intricate details later.
- ✓ They finish it first and then refine it later.

Commit to a hard start and a hard finish from the most complex to the simplest tasks: rolling out a new business, completing a project, doing your hair and makeup, getting the baby ready, working out, or even just making dinner.

Gemstone, hold on to this nugget of wisdom from Sheryl Sandberg: *"Done is better than perfect."*

MARCH 21 GEM
Have substance.

What value do you add to society? Many believe that this is a deep, thought-provoking question, but it really isn't.

How do you contribute to your immediate environment or circle of people? Are you a "me phi me" person who's just sucking the world dry? Or are you influential, inspirational, and creative and someone who gives back, encourages others, and lends a helping hand?

Gemstone, be a woman of substance and don't be self-absorbed. It's about being effective in the space and society you live and operate daily within.

Leave footprints for the next generation to follow! That's your duty.

MARCH 22 GEM

"The days are long, but the years are short."

The above well-recognized quote is accredited to American author Gretchen Rubin. Seasoned mothers share this quote with new mothers. It's an encouraging sentiment for parents.

Parenting can take you through the good, the bad, and the very long and tiring days that sometimes you wish would just hurry up and be done. But as the years go by—which they do!—parents look back and long for those early days again.

Though every minute with your child may not be the most enjoyable, Gemstone, do your best to enjoy those minutes! Appreciate and embrace every moment.

MARCH 23 GEM
Parkinson's Law.

Parkinson's Law says that whatever task you need to complete will expand and extend to fill the time available for its completion. In other words, whatever time you're given to do something, it will take you exactly that amount of time to get it done.

If you're given one hour to get your hair and makeup done, it will take you one hour to get your hair and makeup done. If you give yourself two hours to soak in the bathtub, it will take you two hours to soak in the bathtub. If you have 7 days to read a book, it will take you 7 days to read that book. If you're given 15 days to deliver a project for work, it will take you 15 days to deliver that project for work.

Gemstone, use *Parkinson's Law* to your advantage! Set realistic deadlines, avoid fire drills, stick to your commitments, and be massively productive within your given timeframe.

MARCH 24 GEM
Writers' room.

Gemstone, who's writing your story? This is a serious question.

Who are the writers, producers, and showrunners operating from within you? Who has access to your soul, which is the compilation of your will, mind, and emotions?

Who is brainstorming and pitching ideas for you to act out when you hear the director yell "Lights, camera, action"?

The answer to this question requires self-evaluation. What or who have you allowed to seep into your subconscious that then becomes your script?

Does your inner *writers' room* land you Emmys? Or perhaps may win you an Oscar or a Tony award. Does it put you on the Z-list or worse, have you banned from red carpets?—Yikes!

With the right guidance and direction, take control and be the writer of your own story to win in life.

MARCH 25 GEM
Learn something new.

Gemstone, if you want to learn about business, invest-ments, branding, parenting, international travel, upskill-ing, relationships, etc., you must read about it, research it, and explore it. Most importantly, start applying your newly found knowledge immediately.

Knowledge is not meant to be stagnant! According to author and business expert Josh Kaufman in his "The First 20 Hours" TEDx talk, it only takes about 20 hours to *learn something new.*

To make this work, carve out 20 hours within your selected weekly, biweekly, or monthly time frame and im-merse yourself in learning what you don't know. Choose your cadence and make it work for you.

How?

Create a personal learning plan, then schedule time for learning on your calendar and commit to your plan. Mix up your learnings and stay on topic. If you're learn-ing about marriage, for example, read relevant books, attend marriage workshops, and follow marriage experts online by watching their YouTube videos, listening to their podcasts, and reading their blogs.

MARCH 26 GEM
Elephant in the room.

How can you move forward without discussing the necessary first?

Gemstone, always seek to clear the air and hash out the *elephant in the room* with those who matter.

A controversy amongst the group that is not settled will eventually combust and become a three-alarm fire.

Don't get burned!

MARCH 27 GEM
"You're different."

"Weird," "strange," "odd"... Yeah, you've been called all those things. How complimentary of people to regard you in this manner!

When you're referred to as being "different," that sets you apart from what people have normalized. Truth be told, Gemstone, being different is the best thing to be.

You think differently, you process differently, you see things differently, you challenge the status quo, you go against the grain, people cannot control you, you're irreplaceable, you have people's attention, you're less stressed out, you're creative, you inspire others, you think outside the box, you don't care what others think about you, you're happier, you're unique, you're intriguing, you don't feel restricted, and you're probably rarely bored.

Certainly, *"You're different."*

Embrace the characterization of being different and live up to it!

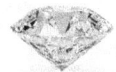

MARCH 28 GEM

Listen to your gut.

Gemstone, what is giving you indigestion, heartburn, constipation, and overall discomfort?

There are many over-the-counter medicines designed to treat all of the above, but it's time to go deeper and figure out the internal issue(s) that may be the real cause of your intestinal problems.

Many people don't realize it, but *stress* can cause tummy issues. According to Netdoctor, psychologists have found links between emotions and stomach issues; many researchers associate anxiety with gut concerns.

If stress—known as "the silent killer"—is the root cause of your discomfort, stop everything and address your source of stress immediately.

Real solutions for addressing deep-seated feelings, life issues, and problems that cause you to stress out may begin in the chair of a mental wellness professional, while symptoms of stress should be treated by a medical doctor.

As the saying goes, *"Listen to your gut."*

MARCH 29 GEM

"What does that have to do with the price of tea in China?"

Is someone else's response completely irrelevant to the statement you just made?

If so, then Gemstone, that's a strong signal that the other person is not listening to you or just doesn't care about what you have to say. They are more concerned with their own agenda and don't know how to hold a balanced conversation where both parties engage with each other's presented topics.

Check people when they advertently try to switch the subject by responding in an irrelevant way and not acknowledging your original statement.

Call them out to stop this rude behavior!

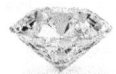

MARCH 30 GEM
Wear a poker face.

Embrace neutrality! Stop being so readable and transparent at board tables.

Stop wearing your feelings on your face. Mask your emotions, Gemstone, when making tough decisions in business settings. Check your facial expressions and command the respect you deserve.

Observe the poker faces displayed by your company's C-suite executives! They wear them for a reason.

Your *poker face* is not a "resting b**" face. It's an "I'm taking business seriously, so respect me" face.

MARCH 31 GEM

For every action, there is a reaction.

According to Newton's Third Law of Motion, the force exerted on one object by another must be returned with a force of equal magnitude and opposite direction. This means that there is a response to every initiated action.

Beyond the realm of physics, when the "objects" are people, many people view this kind of action-followed-by-a-returned-action scenario as being karma. Karma is the principle behind cause and effect.

The Golden Rule of "Do to others as you would have them do to you" and the principles of "You reap what you sow" and "What goes around, comes around" can also be applied here.

Gemstone, watch your actions, because reactions are absolutely guaranteed.

APRIL 1 GEM
Learn how to say "I love you."

Gemstone, is it hard for you to say *"I love you"* to your loved ones?

Do you find yourself saying it only during life's uncertainties, like when the boat is sinking, a loved one's surgery is tomorrow, or a relationship is on its last leg?

Some people cannot verbally express those three words because their silence is learned behavior from their childhood—*"I love you"* was never said in the home or they feel unworthy of receiving love. Or they don't know how to be vulnerable.

If that's you, how can you fix this? *Practice saying "I love you"* to yourself first and believe it when you say it. Become comfortable with saying the words until it feels natural. Then move towards saying *"I love you"* to those you love.

If all else fails, seek professional help to get to the root cause of not being able to verbally communicate your love for someone.

APRIL 2 GEM
You know what to do, so do it.

This is your life, so stop procrastinating! Mind over matter. Mind controls matter. Stop worrying about the "how" and just move forward.

You've contemplated what to do for a long time and you already have several strategies in mind. Move forward with the easiest strategy, Gemstone, and things will begin to fall into place.

You may not have every single resource and tool you need, but start with whatever you do have to set things in motion.

Cast away your fear; cast away your critics; cast away anything and everything that does not align with what you need to get done.

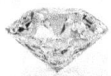

APRIL 3 GEM
Instant success.

Success that comes easily is nice but oftentimes harder to sustain, whereas the success that was achieved by blood, sweat, and tears will last because real work was put in to acquire it.

You are a disciplined person when you work hard for something and continue to keep at it to maintain it.

Congratulations if you stumble upon *instant success,* Gemstone, but work to learn and grow and do everything you need to do to sustain and maximize that success.

APRIL 4 GEM
Grind with a purpose.

A Gemstone who grinds is working hard for hers. She keeps the "pedal to the metal" to get things done.

Many people grind daily:

- ✓ Business owners consistently market their products and services.
- ✓ Shop owners manage their wares and make sales.
- ✓ Commissioned saleswomen are relentless in winning new clients.
- ✓ College students who also work full-time jobs bust their butts.
- ✓ Women are working around the clock to make a living, take care of their families, and have a better life.

Grind with a purpose by ensuring that all the hard work you put in is connected to achieving your lifetime goals.

APRIL 5 GEM
Vibrational energy.

Energy, okaaay!

You are a vibrating mechanism. Rhythms are occurring in the human body and in your body, and those energies generated from within are stimulating chemical processes.

Neurologists continue to make discoveries about and draw connections between the vibrations of our bodies and our thoughts and behaviors.

Practicing yoga is a way to raise your positive *vibrational energy* within your body and rid yourself of negative frequencies.

Namaste, Gemstone.

APRIL 6 GEM
Avoid bad boys.

Women continue to be attracted to men who are reckless, "pushing weight," narcissistic, super-aggressive, excessively dominant, orchestrating and participating in criminal activities, and wreaking havoc.

Women who love these bad boys can't get enough of them.

It's their roughness, toughness, dark personalities, propensity to live on the edge, and willingness to embrace a self-destructive lifestyle that draws women in and makes them moist. (Eye roll...)

It's cute, real cute...until it's not. Until these bad boys become problematic and are turning your world upside down.

> *"Bad boys, bad boys*, what 'cha gonna do, what
> 'cha gonna do when they come for you?"
> —Bob Marley

Gemstone, you better run!

APRIL 7 GEM
The eyes look, but the brain sees.

Your eyes are the informational channels to your brain, while the mind sees everything around you. And according to neuroscience, your mind chooses what it wants to process.

Gemstone, what you perceive to be true is what becomes your reality. Your reality sets your boundaries in life, and your reality is based on what you believe in your mind.

Believe in the constructive, favorable, and positive visions in your head to propel yourself further ahead in life.

APRIL 8 GEM

Your kryptonite.

Whatever *your kryptonite* is, it makes you weak in the knees and deprives you of strength. You give into it (or fall for it) every time, but it's not good for you.

What's *your kryptonite*? Excessive junk food, bad relationships, bad addictions? Kryptonite not only makes you weak but makes you fail.

Gemstone, the time is now to defeat and eliminate *your kryptonite*—the thing that's trying to destroy you.

Like Wonder Woman or any other superhero, use your inner powers and strength to fight back against what's fighting you.

APRIL 9 GEM
Like him.

- ✓ Like him mature.
- ✓ Like him with a career.
- ✓ Like him with a good foundation.
- ✓ Like him with faith.
- ✓ Like him with an education.
- ✓ Like him business-savvy.
- ✓ Like him good with his hands.
- ✓ Like him resourceful.
- ✓ Like him with a 401(k), 403(b), pension, or IRA.
- ✓ Like him with an investment portfolio.
- ✓ Like him independent.
- ✓ Like him drama-free.
- ✓ Like him health-cautious.
- ✓ Like him respectful and kind.

Now that's the way to *like him*, Gemstone!

APRIL 10 GEM

Don't answer everyone's questions.

Gemstone, you are not obligated to answer everyone's questions.

Some people are beyond inquisitive—they are entirely too nosey and have ulterior motives. They don't need to know everything about you.

Leave certain things to their imagination! Let their minds wander. Respectfully, they need to get out of your business, and you need to let them know that.

APRIL 11 GEM
Once a mistake, twice on purpose.

The first time a mistake happens, it's because of a misguided decision on your part to trust a betrayer.

But the second time you kept them around, they had no real remorse for their actions, nor did they present a detailed commitment to change. And you did not establish any rules or boundaries for them to adhere to.

Clearly, you made an informed decision to repeatedly accept their inexcusable behavior without any consequences. Shame.

The first time may have been a mistake, but the second time, that mistake was made with intent.

Gemstone, don't let there be a three-peat.

APRIL 12 GEM
Stop punishing yourself.

- ✓ Stop hating yourself.
- ✓ Stop not living a healthy lifestyle.
- ✓ Stop not getting proper sleep.
- ✓ Stop not getting annual health exams.
- ✓ Stop not taking your mental health seriously.
- ✓ Stop smoking cigarettes.
- ✓ Stop being so lazy.
- ✓ Stop being irresponsible.
- ✓ Stop not holding others accountable.
- ✓ Stop not setting personal goals.
- ✓ Stop expecting others to solve your problems for you.
- ✓ Stop not reading, learning, and growing.
- ✓ Stop being a people pleaser.
- ✓ Stop arriving late and wasting people's time.
- ✓ Stop lying to yourself.
- ✓ Stop normalizing unhealthy relationships.
- ✓ Stop giving up on your faith.

Gemstone, the process of unpunishing yourself begins once you stop.

APRIL 13 GEM
Embrace reciprocity.

Feed what feeds you. If people are investing in you, your family, and your business and you are not feeding, giving, acknowledging, thanking, and appreciating them in return, then you are using people.

Stop being inconsiderate of the time that others invest in you. How greedy, selfish, and unthankful can you be? Where's the reciprocity in that type of behavior?

Gemstone, no one owes you anything except to love you (Rom. 13:8), and that's free. This self-absorbing behavior is tiring.

People are cutting ties with those who are selfish—because who really wants to feel used all the time?

Where and how in your friendships, relationships, and business dealings can you be more reciprocal?

APRIL 14 GEM
Dancing in the rain.

Don't allow life's hiccups to deter you from pressing ahead.

Life is filled with ups and downs, but don't stop performing those eight-counts when showers fall from the sky.

Enjoy the journey, Gemstone…"and a 5, 6, 7, 8…"

APRIL 15 GEM
Rest.

Get the proper *rest* and sleep your body needs, because your body organs need downtime.

Gemstone, you're a hardworking woman who deserves a break. Pick a day every 6 to 8 days to just do absolutely nothing or to do the bare minimum to allow your body to recover.

Relax and reenergize today so that you can show up even better tomorrow.

Your body is counting on you—So *rest* well!

APRIL 16 GEM
Do it moving!

You're constantly thinking about making a change, but every day you push the goalpost further and further out because you keep delaying your start date. Whatever you desire to get done, change, or accomplish in life, *do it moving* and remember that nothing has to be perfectly positioned for you to start making changes.

Haven't had the time to clean the junk foods out of your pantry so that you can start your new healthy lifestyle? *Do it moving!* Begin increasing your daily vegetable intake and decreasing your intake of simple carbs while simultaneously ridding your pantry of junk whenever you can.

Want to start your own business but you're not in a position to quit your current job? *Do it moving!* Work your regular 9-to-5 and begin working on the small things you need to do to start forming your business during your lunch breaks. Dedicate an additional 30 minutes to an hour to building your empire each evening when you get home.

Want to write and publish a book but can't find time to sit down and write it? *Do it moving!* Use a writing app on your phone and start writing your manuscript everywhere you go whenever you can, even if only for a few minutes a day. Watch how quickly the pages and chapters begin to add up. You'll be publishing your book before you know it.

Stop wasting hidden time, Gemstone, and *do it moving!*

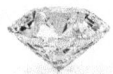

APRIL 17 GEM
No choice is a choice.

"I don't have a choice," you say.

Someone around the globe is cueing their violin to this fatuity, because settling on not having a choice is your choice.

Many people do not grasp the depths of the statement that *"no choice is a choice"* right away, so Gemstone, repeat it until it truly sinks in.

APRIL 18 GEM
Walk away.

- ✓ Walk away from bad relationships.
- ✓ Walk away from toxic people.
- ✓ Walk away from procrastinators.
- ✓ Walk away from Debbie Downers.
- ✓ Walk away from those who throw rocks and then hide their hands.
- ✓ Walk away from cheaters.
- ✓ Walk away from liars.
- ✓ Walk away from time wasters.
- ✓ Walk away from haters.
- ✓ Walk away from unproductive people.
- ✓ Walk away from doubleminded individuals.
- ✓ Walk away from users.

These types of people are not always easy to *walk away* from because of the time you invested in them knowingly or unknowingly of their true character—it's hard as hell to walk away from an investment. But the investment is bad, and you know it.

Gemstone, when there is no return on your investment, *walk away.*

APRIL 19 GEM
Straight, no chaser.

Like a shot of Patrón unaccompanied by a mixer, sometimes the best way to "take it" is straight.

Gemstone, if you can face the hard realities in life unsugarcoated and not dressed up—if you can take those realities exactly as they are—you are a very strong individual.

People will then know that they do not have to soften the blow when relaying information to you because you are tenacious and can swallow what's being served without chewing.

Facing unadulterated facts allows you to handle tough issues more efficiently. Stop receiving information that's been watered down! Instead, ask for the unfiltered version.

Get to the core of whatever it is by taking it *straight, no chaser* so that you can handle things more quickly and effectively.

APRIL 20 GEM
Know your philosophy.

Understanding the fundamental truths about yourself, your beliefs, your whys in life, your relationships, and your connections to this world and this society forms your philosophy.

Your philosophy, Gemstone, should go beyond your assumptions to reel in your truths behind the whys and ways in which you think and act.

Now put on your Ph.D. cap and delve into the philosophy of your life!

APRIL 21 GEM

Prove it.

Gemstone, considering a relationship? Make him prove himself to you.

His actions need to demonstrate that he is worth such a commitment, that he deserves your love and your time, and that he is entitled to your devotion.

If he can't prove himself, then you shouldn't commit, because he's not worth your love, time, and loyalty—all things that come with commitment.

Do not make this hard for yourself! Adhere to this guidance and save yourself from unnecessary heartache and pain.

APRIL 22 GEM
What's it all for?

It's nice to save and have your stashed-away coins for rainy days.

However, *what's it all for* if you never spend it? Your savings should be tied to a purpose.

Saving money all your life without any specific reason for it is ridiculous. Have a plan for your funds and never feel guilty for wanting to spend a little of what you've saved to enjoy life's pleasures.

Gemstone, save for life's surprises (good or bad) save for fun days, save for achieving your dreams, save for retirement, save for your children, save to give to worthy causes, save to help others, save to pass down your savings to your future generations as an inheritance.

Whatever it's for, make it all be for something.

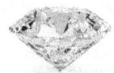

APRIL 23 GEM

Enrich your phone apps.

Gemstone, if someone were to open your phone and conduct an audit of your apps, what would they see? Instagram, Facebook, TikTok, YouTube, Triller, Apple TV+, Pinterest, Twitter, People, TMZ, Target, Amazon, Disney+, Netflix, eBay, or WhatsApp?

From those apps alone, the auditor would be able to tell a lot about your personality and the amount of entertainment and social interaction you engage in— essentially, the auditor would know what you're influenced by. What's missing from your installed apps? Potentially opportunities for core learning, growing, and self-development.

It's time to diversify and expand your phone app repertoire with apps pertaining to continuous learning, global news, tech, investments, spiritual growth, and health and wellness. These kinds of apps can help you enhance your knowledge and skills.

Download some of the following apps to your phone to increase your learning and growth, personal development, and health and wellness: Audible, Skillshare, Bloomberg, Investor's, Forbes, Business Daily, Babbel, MyFitnessPal, Tandem, BetterMe, Flo, Khan Academy, 365 Gratitude Journal, Udemy Business, LinkedIn, edX, Amazon Kindle, Financial Times, Ancestry DNA, Bible Gateway, and Visit A City.

APRIL 24 GEM
Turn your lessons into wins.

Gemstone, every lesson is an opportunity to use what you've learned to help you succeed in life.

Every lesson provides you with new knowledge that you did not previously have. With your new knowledge comes responsibility—lessons learned are teachings, ideas, and principles that you can use to develop yourself.

Every lesson learned puts you on a higher playing field if and only if you apply the lesson, in turn upping your own personal baseline. Every time you put into action what you've learned, you're winning.

Wins from lessons are only wins if what was learned is carried out by the learner.

Turn your lessons into wins by carrying out what you've learned! Otherwise, you've only gained information.

APRIL 25 GEM
You will...

- ✓ You will self-reflect.
- ✓ You will focus.
- ✓ You will take responsibility.
- ✓ You will hold others accountable.
- ✓ You will stop overspending.
- ✓ You will eat healthier.
- ✓ You will work out.
- ✓ You will set boundaries.
- ✓ You will make better life decisions.
- ✓ You will meditate and pray.
- ✓ You will honor your temple (your body).
- ✓ You will be grateful.
- ✓ You will seek knowledge.
- ✓ You will seek wisdom.
- ✓ You will seek power, respectfully.
- ✓ You will be better.
- ✓ You will try your hardest.
- ✓ You will not give up.
- ✓ You will reward yourself for small wins.

Gemstone, *you will* enjoy this day.

APRIL 26 GEM
Died at 30, buried at 75.

When things don't happen exactly when you want them to, it doesn't mean they won't happen—it just means it's not your time. Either there's something better for you right now or you need to focus on doing something else for the time being.

So don't die at age 30 and sit dormant doing nothing until…well…you croak and are finally buried at 75 by your friends and family.

That's 45 years of waste!

That's 45 years of you sucking up oxygen for no reason!

That's 45 years of you whining, complaining, and working the nerves of others, more than likely because you didn't get your way in life and you did nothing about that.

You didn't get busy working on another goal; you didn't get busy helping others reach theirs; you didn't get busy coming up with an alternative plan; you didn't get busy tapping into your other gifts and talents. Essentially, you weren't busy at all.

Deciding to do nothing else in life because of an un-manifested goal or dream is for the weak-minded, which you are not. You are strong-minded!

For every door closed, open the next one. For every dream delayed, reach for the low-hanging fruit. Every time someone tells you "No," say "Yes!" to something else. For every step you take back, take two more steps forward.

Gemstone, don't expire when you're internally young! Live your life to the fullest, every moment and every day.

APRIL 27 GEM
Transactional love.

Ka-ching! Ka-ching! Ka-ching!

That's the sound of the cash register collecting your sales.

You paid for the dinner, dessert, movies, and gas. Then somewhere after "hello" and a few months in, you started paying his rent, utilities, car note, and God knows what else. Now you're babysitting his snotty-nosed kids while staying up late to see what wee hour of the morning he'll arrive back home.

What you thought was love is one-sided *transactional love.*

This non-example of a man is getting everything he possibly can in exchange for very little on his end. He reaps all the benefits at your expense and will continue to string you along if you let him.

And why not? As the saying goes, "Why buy the cow when the milk is free?"

Gemstone, this is not a relationship! It's not even a partnership. It's a financial takeover of your pockets and emotions.

As Tyra Banks says, cut your losses now and "Learn from this!"

APRIL 28 GEM
Teach her the business.

Give a woman a job, and she'll earn a paycheck, but *teach a woman the business*, and she'll run the company. Gemstone, teaching is greater than giving.

APRIL 29 GEM
"What a time to be alive."

The first woman says, "Despite all the many issues and problems in this world, *what a time to be alive.* I have access, I have power, and I am making the generations before and after me proud."

The second woman says, *"What a time to be alive...* there are so many global issues and problems and no good left in humanity! What really is there to do in life?"

"What a time to be alive" is an ambiguous statement since such rhetoric can carry such different convictions for different people—for some, it's incredibly positive; for others, it's negative. Gemstone, how do you feel about that statement?

The first woman has a very hopeful outlook and therefore future, but the second woman doesn't, because her inner thoughts reveal that she's already given up.

Like the first woman does, the second woman unknowingly holds the key to her own destiny, too.

APRIL 30 GEM
No impact is too small.

To think that lil' ol' you, Gemstone, don't add value, have no influence, and serve no purpose is such a low thought.

Examine the mosquito and its impact. Look how much ruckus and chaos that tiny insect causes when it's in a room full of people!

If the likes of a tiny mosquito can have that much impact, then truly how much more impactful can you be?

The answer is "Very!"

MAY 1 GEM
It be your own people.

Sometimes, it's the ones closest to you who hurt you the most.

You thought they were on your side and that you had their support, but you thought wrong. Even Jesus himself was not supported by some of his own (John 1:11).

Gemstone, some of your own people may not support your new business venture, while others who are close may not congratulate you on major accomplishments.

10 reasons why "your own" may not support you:

1.   They don't believe in you or endorse what you're doing.
2.   They can't see "you" beyond who or how you used to be.
3.   They don't understand who you are and what your brand is.
4.   They are jealous and envious or insecure.
5.   They are interested only in their current relationship dynamics with you and not your evolution.
6.   They have a different status level, faith, or mindset.
7.   They're afraid of how their relationship with you may change.

8.   You're involved in too many things and support-
     ing you is overwhelming and exhausting.
9.   They're busy themselves with their own projects.
10. They have other life circumstances that have
     nothing to do with you that they need to focus on.

Do not get into the weeds of why they won't support you—that's a waste of time. You don't have to stop loving them, but depending on the situation, loving them from a distance may be best.

Always keep in mind that your endorsers, followers and supporters may come from outside your inner circle. You just might be pleasantly surprised.

MAY 2 GEM
Show them the receipts.

When people try to gaslight you to play on your emotions—when they act as if something hasn't happened that quite clearly did—then roll out the receipts.

Hold onto your receipts when you have to deal with shady people. Receipts are hard evidence that keeps the opposition in their proper place when you have to check them.

People are quick to forget what they said or did, but that's nothing that a saved screenshot, tweet, picture, voicemail, email, or video can't prove.

Your receipts, Gemstone, are your evidence. They are the proof you can use to deter others from violating and assassinating your character.

Receipts are becoming more and more necessary in this digital world and they are admissible in court.

Talk is still cheap, but receipts are worth every dime.

Silence them with your receipts.

MAY 3 GEM
Don't be petty.

Gemstone, it's not even worth your time.

Why are you giving so much attention to something so trivial and unimportant? Your pettiness is at an all-time high. More than likely, you're probably "loud and wrong" anyway.

Turn down the undue concern and trivial behavior by not making a big deal out of everything. Don't play the victim in every situation and don't try to be "right" all the time. Even if you are right, what does that change? Nothing.

Stop being super judgy of others. Stop being condescending and passive-aggressive. Stop feeling the need to have the final word every time.

Stop being petty.

MAY 4 GEM
Obvious to others.

You are so self-critical that it's too hard for you to see just how wonderful, beautiful, and talented you are...but it's *obvious to others.*

They see your greatness, they see your potential, they see your talents. Gemstone, your wonderfulness is very apparent to them because they see you in the light that you should also be seeing yourself in.

The self-deprecating words you tell yourself and the unrealistic high expectations you put on yourself severely mask how great you are.

You need to truly believe in yourself. Ask others exactly what they see in you that makes you so great and write down those qualities.

Look for the commonalities in the good things that people say about you, because that's where your flourishing character shines the most. Reflect daily on what's been shared with you. Repeat those good words in your affirmations (refer to your January 31 Gem), add them to your mantra, and meditate on all that's good about you.

See it, believe it, and own it, because you are great!

MAY 5 GEM

Silence is golden.

The saying *"silence is golden"* has won many battles as well as prevented many wars.

Holding your tongue when you're very angry will preserve your relationships.

Holding your tongue will cease arguments, because the other person cannot argue alone.

Holding your tongue will save you from saying something you will regret.

Knowing how to speak and communicate your words eloquently is powerful, but Gemstone, the virtue of your silence will send shockwaves.

MAY 6 GEM

Pros versus cons.

The Latin phrase *pro et contra* or *"pros versus cons"* is an ancient method for weighing decisions, and it's still very effective today.

You need to weigh the costs of your potential decisions by listing the effects of your presented options.

Be clear in what your arguments are in favor of a decision. Be clear in what your arguments are against a decision. Gemstone, this is one of the core tenets of effective decision-making.

The obvious decision reveals itself when "pen is to paper," so to speak—you'll see that one column winds up being longer than the other.

MAY 7 GEM
Loosen your grip.

Personal trainers often tell weightlifters to *loosen their grip* on the weights they're trying to lift in the gym. Why? Because *loosening their grip* allows them to lift more.

Holding a weight too tightly places an incredible amount of stress and pain on your wrists that can shoot up to your forearms and tire you out, making you unable to lift anything else. The same can be applied to the challenges you're facing in life.

What problems or issues do you need to *loosen your grip* on? Where in life are you being so hard on yourself that you're causing yourself stress and emotional pain? Where are you making it unbearable to handle even the normal things in life?

Gemstone, *loosen your grip* by releasing your problems and issues that are mentally exhausting.

Give your problems to your higher power. Ask for help, seek therapy, and let go of other people's problems—after all, they were never yours to begin with.

MAY 8 GEM
Know your nonnegotiables.

Gemstone, it's imperative to establish what you will and won't accept when dating someone and before becoming exclusive with them.

Your boundaries should be clearly defined and communicated to the other person before you make any kind of personal commitment. Sticking to *your relationship nonnegotiables* helps protect you from being emotionally violated and mistreated.

Your line in the sand sets the precedent that you love and respect yourself and will not compromise your values.

Your partner must oblige you by adhering to *your nonnegotiables* if they want to be in a committed relationship with you.

Respect, faith, love, loyalty, morality, family, and finances are just a few examples of nonnegotiables you should consider establishing before you commit to a serious relationship and jump the broom.

MAY 9 GEM
Don't say "Do it better."

Gemstone, it's time to rephrase your words to improve your outcomes.

If your significant other didn't clean the kitchen in a way that meets the standards of your home or they didn't repair a broken item or handle a situation correctly, *don't tell them to "do it better."* Instead, ask them to "do it differently."

Asking them to "do it better" is really asking them to repeat the same actions by getting better at not meeting your desired standards for a performed task.

Therefore, it's best to ask them to "do it differently"— then they can make the connection that they need to make changes to the way they're currently doing something in order to have an improved outcome.

MAY 10 GEM
Have skin in the game.

When investing in stocks, you *have skin in the game.* When making business deals, you *have skin in the game.* When getting a loan, you *have skin in the game.* When getting married, you *have skin in the game.* When having children, you *have skin in the game.*

Having skin in the game drives your accountability because there's something to lose if you are irresponsible.

Gemstone, be leery of those with no *skin in the game!* They have nothing to lose and may not care about those who do.

MAY 11 GEM
Fail fast, fail forward, fail often.

Some of the most successful and well-known women— Lucille Ball, Vera Wang, Oprah Winfrey, Marilyn Monroe, Ruth Fertel, Viola Davis, J.K. Rowling—*failed fast, failed forward, and failed often.*

People who try, fail. Then they get back up and try again and they continue to rework whatever they're working on until they succeed. As the saying goes, "If you haven't failed, you haven't tried."

In the gym, athletes work their bodies and muscles to failure daily. They have consistent discipline and they push themselves farther each time. That's when they begin to see serious gains.

The same goes for whatever you're trying to accomplish in life—there will be a lot of failures, but the key is to fail fast every time, meaning that you get back up right away and keep going. Failing fast makes you stronger and more resilient.

Gemstone, try again! Go farther and farther each time and keep trying. When you keep at it, your failures will begin to work in your favor and you will come to see that you're truly pressing forward more and more. So, be inspired by those who dusted themselves off, rolled up their sleeves, and never allowed their failures to stop them from trying.

MAY 12 GEM
Taking the test.

Some moments in life may leave you feeling lonely or scared, like when you're facing obstacles. You may even feel abandoned by God, your parents, close friends, and others...but that may not necessarily be what's happening.

Think for a moment—some of those same people have prepared, reared, and guided you and instilled in you all of the skills, tools, guidance, wisdom, and know-how you need to overcome life's biggest tests.

When faced with difficult challenges, it's always good to remember that the teacher is silent when you're *taking the test*.

Cheers to you in advance, Gemstone, for passing every test in life with flying colors!

MAY 13 GEM
The phone works both ways.

The next time a friend or family member tries to make you feel bad by saying, "I haven't heard from you in a long time," let them know that *the phone works both ways* and is the same distance from one end to the other.

Life is busy enough for people, especially for those working vigorously towards their goals while they're also handling their other day-to-day responsibilities such as going to work, taking care of their children, and catering to their spouse.

People need to respect that there's no love lost but that you also have priorities you must tend to.

Don't allow others to shame you for not calling them often. Instead, Gemstone, agree on a communication cadence that works for both of you to improve the relationship and then stick to it.

MAY 14 GEM

"I go drink water and mind my business."

Trinidadian soca singer Patrice Roberts says it best in "Mind My Business" when she sings *"I go drink water and mind my business."* Stop worrying about what other people are doing! If they want you to know, they will tell you.

Gemstone, you have enough going on in your own life—you don't need to be concerned with the four corners of other people's homes that literally have nothing to do with you.

Stop inserting yourself into others' situations. Stop calling around and gossiping. Stop giving your opinion when no one asked.

Go ahead and sing it now: *"I go drink water and mind my business."*

MAY 15 GEM

Beware those who divide and conquer.

Have you allowed someone into your inner circle or relationship who then lit a torch and destroyed it?

They disturbed the inner dynamics by pitting one person against the another, resulting in the demise of the friendship or relationship. But then even as the culprit, they came out unscathed, unbothered, and in control. Like a dictator, they mastered dividing and conquering, a cynical and calculated power move.

Why would you give someone the power to destroy your friendships and relationships? What was their ulterior motive for creating division? What did they get out of it?

Gemstone, it's time to take back control! Expose the master manipulator and remove them from your life.

If they're repairable, work on mending broken friendships and relationships that suffered from the deceptive workings of an external party who had a hidden agenda.

MAY 16 GEM

"Do you want me to listen, or do you want my thoughts?"

That is one of the best questions to ask when someone comes to you baring their problems.

Oftentimes, you may assume that people are interested in your feedback and guidance...but that may very well not be the case.

Gemstone, people do not always want answers or solutions. They might just want you to listen to them and maybe even console them. Providing them with a solution is not always what's best since allowing them to organically arrive at their own resolution helps them learn and grow.

Find out the role they need you to play in that moment. This is one of the best ways to provide emotional support to those who are counting on you.

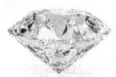

MAY 17 GEM
Extend your hand.

Someone took a chance on you, Gemstone.

They gave you an opportunity that no one else was willing to give you and that opportunity completely changed your life.

How can you *extend your hand* today and help someone else become one step closer to achieving their dreams?

MAY 18 GEM
Do the grunt work.

Sometimes you just have to get your hands dirty and *do the grunt work.*

Starting off in an entry-level role at an organization and working your way up is not only a humbling experience but a teachable one.

Your experience and career trajectory within a firm speak volumes. Mastering different levels and roles at a company makes you a value-added employee and inspires others to follow in your footsteps.

Many CEOs have followed this route: they started in a low-ranking position and within time became the CEO of the company.

Do not despise humble beginnings, Gemstone! Don't deplore grunt work, because it's the humble beginnings that keep you grounded when you get to the top.

MAY 19 GEM
Your browser history.

Inspect *your browser history*. What sites have you visited in the last 30 days? Your web history reveals your mindset and where most of your focus has been.

If at least 30% to 50% of *your browser history* has not been tied to achieving your goals, figure out how it can be moving forward.

Identify what needs to change. What do you need to be doing more of to get closer to reaching your goals?

This is not a drill! Nor is it a game.

It's time to cut the foolishness, Gemstone, and get serious about the work you need to do so that you can live the life you've always dreamed of.

MAY 20 GEM
The power of meaning.

The English word "crisis" means "opportunity" in Chinese.

The Chinese do not view crises as problems the same way that Americans do. Intelligently, the Chinese develop solutions by creating businesses and jobs to address their opportunities. This is a smart way for them to generate income and wealth.

Think about the personal words in your vocabulary that have negative connotations to them, like "problems," "issues," and "chaos."

Then, Gemstone, flip those words into "answers," "resolutions," and "systemization" to change your thinking and approach.

Turn your problems into business opportunities that generate promising and unlimited possibilities.

MAY 21 GEM
Not on my watch!

Gemstone, be bold about what will not be happening while you are in charge.

You are in control of your life, and as long as you are in control, time thieves, dream snatchers, procrastinators, and unproductive energy wasters *will not be on your watch*.

Set precedents with yourself and others up front about what you will and will not tolerate.

MAY 22 GEM
Never chase an AWOL.

If he's gone, he's gone.

He left for a reason and typically without notice.

When a man walks away from a relationship without cause, yes, you are entitled to know why...but you need to determine whether he's worth pursuing or even knowing.

Unless he's battling deep-seated, family, or health-related issues that you're aware of, let him go! Because Gemstone, he is showing you exactly who he is.

This person is toxic and wants to see how much they have you wrapped around their finger by making you chase them—making you pursue them is a form of manipulation and control. They don't want to be in a relationship with you anymore but don't know how to tell you that. How cowardly! They are hiding something from you; their habit of randomly disappearing keeps you from learning the truth.

A man who knows what he wants doesn't play a disappearing act to make a woman chase him. If a man respects and values you, he won't just vanish into thin air.

Never chase an AWOL! When you don't, that AWOL will quickly learn that you love and respect yourself, that you know your worth, and that your self-dignity ranks above their antics.

MAY 23 GEM
Inaction gets you nowhere.

Get off your hind parts and do something, because *inaction gets you nowhere.*

How can you become a top podcaster without writing your show's script, recording it, and posting it to various podcast platforms? How can you achieve your goal by only thinking about it?

How can you become a top influencer without showcasing various products and services online, tagging them, promoting their products to your followers, and connecting with those companies for brand ambassador opportunities?

How can you sell your skincare products without creating a website, setting up a merchant account, working with a manufacturer and distributor, and promoting your business via social media?

Gemstone, how can you do anything by only sitting around and thinking about it and not putting forth any concrete action?

MAY 24 GEM
Not your story to tell.

Just because you know what happened doesn't mean that it's okay to share that story with others.

Not everything is your story to tell.

Protect the life challenges and mishaps of others. Allow those you love and care about to learn and grow without experiencing judgment from everyone else. Wasn't the mishap enough for them all on its own?

Gemstone, let inquiring minds know that it's *not your story to tell.* If and when the person is ready to tell their story, they will.

MAY 25 GEM
Find your source of insecurity.

Gemstone, it's time to pinpoint the reasons why you don't feel confident or assured in life so that you can address those insecurities and become a better person. Insecurities hold you back from living out your dreams.

Did you try to lose weight and fail? Are you socially awkward? Are you too hard on yourself?

All of these reasons could be the source of your self-doubt.

Feelings of insecurity are tied to recent failure or rejection, social anxiety, and/or perfectionism according to Clinical Psychologist and life coach, Melanie Greenberg, in her 2015 *Psychology Today* article, "The 3 Most Common Causes of Insecurity and How to Beat Them."

To overcome an insecurity, you must first *determine the source of that insecurity*, recognize that you are worthy, prioritize what's important, and overcome whatever once broke your confidence (criticism, rejection, etc.). And you need to cease looking for anyone else's approval but your own.

If you struggle with getting to the root cause of your insecurity, seeking professional help may be your best solution.

MAY 26 GEM
Finstagram.

Do you have this inner you that no one knows about? Is there something you want to keep private or restrict to sharing with a small, carefully selected group of people?

Cool! Then be just like the celebs and openly express yourself with a "Finsta" (or fake/secret) social media page—then you won't attract the judgment of others.

You, Gemstone, have the same right to let your hair down discreetly online as those celebs do.

MAY 27 GEM
Quick solutions.

With just a push of a few buttons on your phone, it instantly connects to satellites to pinpoint your current location. From there, your phone can take you to your desired destination, giving you vocal directions turn by turn. The days are long gone when you had to read an actual map before taking a trip.

Just like Google Maps has done for drivers, society searches for *quick solutions* to its problems. Going through a process that will help mold you and give you the life skills, tenacity, know-how, and experience you need for your own development is becoming unheard of nowadays.

Why on earth would you want to go through the emotional aftermath of a failed relationship when you can pull out your phone and quickly jump into the next relationship just by "swiping right?"

Examine your life and see where you need to take some serious time to develop, improve, or heal. The quick solution is not always the best one or even an adequate one.

Especially when the pieces that make up your soul are hurt—your heart, mind, will, and emotions—Gemstone, you'll require more than an instant solution.

MAY 28 GEM
Gain perspective.

Gemstone, wise people seek the opinions, facts, and experiences of others. They participate in diversity of thought and are respected because they allow others to be and feel heard.

When you *gain perspectives*, data, and facts, you can make sound decisions while being supported by those you consulted during the process.

Always keep an open mind! After all, more than one truth, more than one way, and more than one solution can coexist.

MAY 29 GEM
Get in front of it first.

Don't allow others to use your truth against you! *Get in front of it first.* Control your narrative, Gemstone, by controlling the story from the beginning.

If there's a potentially embarrassing, shameful, fall-from-grace, or scandalous story about you that you know will get out, get in front of it quickly.

"Out yourself" first to take away the sting from someone else trying to put a more salacious or hurtful version of the story out there. People tend to sympathize more with victims of failure, personal embarrassment, and grief.

Besides, nowadays, nine times out of ten, no matter what happened, someone has recorded it, screenshotted it, or captured it on camera.

Telling your "truth" before anyone else can diminish a lot of the hype in case others do attempt to expose you or tell a different, more exaggerated version of the story.

MAY 30 GEM
Own your "ish."

It's time to *own your "ish" and* stop blaming others for your problems.

You are the only constant in your problems. It is not always someone else's fault. Neither are you immune from making mistakes and doing less-than-credible things just like anyone else would do.

Gemstone, you are a human being, and that's what human beings do: they make mistakes.

There is a strong linkage between those who don't take accountability and narcissists.

Recognize your own actions and make yourself re-proachable and coachable.

Most importantly, *own your "ish!"*

MAY 31 GEM
10 reasons why you are a champion.

1. You are a champion because you wake up every morning feeling grateful, goal-oriented, disciplined, driven, and focused.
2. You are a champion because you are honest with yourself and you face your fears.
3. You are a champion because you are a great student and teacher of your craft.
4. You are a champion because not only do you focus on the present, you think about and act for the future.
5. You are a champion because you use the criticism of others to fuel yourself and push yourself to success.
6. You are a champion because you don't accept "no" the first time someone tells you "no."
7. You are a champion because you take your health and fitness seriously.
8. You are a champion because you are tapped into your God-given talents and gifts.
9. You are a champion because you do not allow your circumstances to stop you from pushing yourself forward.
10. You are a champion because you never give up.

Gemstone, *you are a champion!*

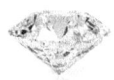

JUNE 1 GEM
It ruffles your feathers.

Are you bothered by what's happening or not happening? Are you ignited by irritation and rage? Do you feel compelled to do something about what upsets you in this world?

When something vehemently bothers you to your core, it's a sign that you need to do something about it. The reason you're so disturbed by it is because you want to fix it or make it better.

Are you extremely annoyed by the lack of manners displayed by today's youth? Then maybe writing a children's book about manners and pitching it to public school systems is one of your callings. Are you disgusted by the laziness of others? Then maybe becoming a motivational speaker or life coach is the work you should be doing. Are you tired of the lack of healthier food options within your community? Then maybe opening or investing in the development of an organic restaurant or grocery store in your area is something that you should be doing.

Whatever it is that consistently *ruffles your feathers,* Gemstone, more than likely you have the perfect solution for it and the ability to start putting your solution into action—in turn changing things for the better, making something of yourself, and creating business opportunities and generating wealth.

JUNE 2 GEM
It's okay to walk away.

Gemstone, walk away from toxic people, toxic relationships, liars, past mistakes, and anything else that stunts your growth. Walk away from laziness, hate, whatever negates your God-given purpose, things and people that consume your time, overspending, financial irresponsibility, immaturity, not taking your mental health seriously, and people who don't believe in you.

Walk away from self-doubt, haters, bad advice, self-criticism, poor mindsets, being worried about what others think, ungrateful people, negativity, overexplaining yourself, trying to convince others, confusion, and anything else that hinders you from achieving your goals.

It's always okay to walk away.

(Refer to the April 18th Gem)

JUNE 3 GEM
Triggered.

At some point in your life, you may have experienced trauma or some kind of negative emotional response to a terrible event. And now, even though the event is in the distant past, occasionally the traumatic experience resurfaces because you are *triggered* by something that stirs your memories.

Being *triggered* affects people's emotional states. Some may experience anxiety, distress, rage, apprehension, and fear as a result.

Gemstone, take control of your life by taking your mental health seriously.

Psychotherapist, David Richo, recommends calling out your *triggers* so that you can stay on your guard and respond to them consciously versus impulsively in his "13 Strategies to Deal with Your Emotional Triggers" in his *Experience Life 2020* piece. This will also allow you to identify the origin of your *triggers* and thus significantly reduce their impact.

Most importantly, seek professional help for managing your *triggers*.

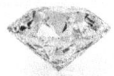

JUNE 4 GEM
Who you used to be.

Stop allowing people to remind you of *who you used to be.* You are not that same person anymore.

Like a bud to a rose, a caterpillar to a butterfly, a princess to a queen, Gemstone, you have evolved.

Inform them that *who you used to be* was your past and that this is who you are now.

Tell them to meet you at who you are today and to leave *who you used to be* in the distant past.

JUNE 5 GEM
Inside itself.

Have you ever taken notice that the seed of a thing is *inside itself* (Gen. 1:11)?

The seed of an apple is *inside itself.* So are the seeds of avocados and oranges and all other fruits and living things. Essentially, every seed produces a "gift."

The apple is sweet and delicious, while the avocado is packed with healthy fats and antioxidants and oranges are loaded with vitamin C. These are their gifts and purposes for those who partake in them. The same goes for you.

Everything you are meant to be in life is already inside of you. To win in life, you just need to identify those things, cultivate them, put them to use for the benefit of others, and continue to refine them.

Don't look outside of yourself to discover your gift, because you won't find it there. You were born with your gift, your talent, your natural aptitude, your skill. You have everything you need right inside of you to be your best self!

Gemstone, you will never find your natural-born gift externally—you will only find it internally. And once you discover your gift, put it to use, because it will allow you to prosper (Prov. 18:16).

JUNE 6 GEM
Okay...so when?

You have all the excuses in the world as to why you have not started to pursue your dreams. At this point, given all your excuses, it looks like you'll never get started.

The time you say you don't have does exist. That time exists within the sacrifices you decide to make.

Sacrifice not going out; stay up one hour later; save money by making your own meals at home; stay on hold that extra 30 minutes to get the answers you need; buy the equipment you need to start your new business versus buying new outfits; wake up one hour earlier every day to give yourself more time to pursue your goals.

Gemstone, when you make sacrifices, that's when you can begin making headway in achieving your dreams.

JUNE 7 GEM
"Put me in, Coach!"

Gemstone, sometimes you just have to let others know that you're ready.

Ask for more responsibilities and take on new challenges. Let your execs know it's time to put you in the starting lineup of the team.

Show them what you got!

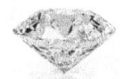

JUNE 8 GEM
Humblebragging.

There's nothing wrong with a little bit of self-admiration, but keep it modest.

Being subtle is key. Humbly share your wins and successes in life occasionally and not excessively.

Gemstone, understand that no matter how rare and random you are about sharing your accomplishments, not everyone will take a liking to them.

Why? Because your *humblebragging* disturbs their souls.

Your social media posts and group sharing may be a reminder of their failures or what they're not accomplishing in life. And some people just won't care about your wins in life due to their own issues and hang-ups or even narcissism.

Brag humbly.

JUNE 9 GEM
Find balance.

People have so much going on that having *balance* in life can be easier said than done.

Maintaining equilibrium in the midst of family responsibilities, relationships, dating, parenting, career aspirations, bills, house chores and upkeep, and friendships—all while trying to achieve your goals—can be quite overwhelming, especially when you don't have help.

The woman who's burned out yet doesn't show tiredness and is somehow still managing everything (and not asking for help) may have what psychologists refer to as "Superwoman Syndrome."

In her 2020 article titled "What is Superwoman Syndrome?" issued by *Step to Health,* philosopher Isbelia Esther Farías López points out the need to acknowledge that you are human. You need to put aside the urge to control everything! Keep in mind that everyone is accountable for their own life and delegate some tasks. Those are a few ways to help you treat this syndrome.

Gemstone, if you think you may have Superwoman Syndrome or you need *balance* in your life, it's an opportune time to consider working with a life coach. A life coach is a wellness professional who will help you create healthy *balance* in your life—together, you'll develop a personalized plan that will allow you to be more intentional about achieving your goals while still creating stability around life's inescapable responsibilities.

JUNE 10 GEM
Go beyond your zip code.

Go beyond your zip code. See what else is out there past your comfort zone.

Gemstone, let this serve as the confirmation you've been looking for—it's the green light to make that move, take that trip, and expand your horizons.

JUNE 11 GEM
Put a simple plan into action.

Health and physical education have always been part of your core curricula, from your primary education years up to college.

You were being taught to have a healthy lifestyle in the hopes that good food and exercise habits would stick with you for a lifetime, reducing the chance of you becoming a long-term patient of your private sector or governmental healthcare system. If you want to live a long life, "Hut, 1, 2, 3, 4!" And get your butt in the gym and eat cleaner. Your healthy lifestyle is a nonnegotiable and does not have to be perfect. You just need to *put a simple plan into action* and not overthink it.

If you struggle with incorporating healthy habits into your daily routine or you need professional guidance, connect with a nutritionist or dietician to help you figure out a strategy that's geared specifically to you.

More employer wellness programs and health insurance policies are covering these types of specialists in their healthcare plans these days. Check with your employer and health insurance provider to see what's available to you.

Gemstone, remember, healthy living is a lifestyle! It requires you to take things one day at a time. Some days will be easy and some days will be hard, but never give up!

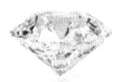

JUNE 12 GEM
Make it enough.

How on earth did your ancestors survive with bare minimums? No TV, no phone, no microwave, no refrigerator, no car, no alarm, no radio...

Whatever you have now, use it, *make it enough* for now, and build on it.

If your ancestors had the ability to be resourceful with so little, how much more resourceful can you be given what you have today?

History shows that it's in your DNA to survive by making use of what you do have. And there are plenty of resources to help you acquire just about anything or everything you lack or currently don't have: food, shelter, clothes, TVs, laptops, cell phones, Wi-Fi, beds, furniture, jobs, childcare, healthcare, continued education, and more.

Make it enough, Gemstone! And then build on it.

JUNE 13 GEM

Mirror, mirror...

"*Mirror, mirror*, on the wall, who's the fairest of them all?"
    "You are!" Believe it.
    "You are!" Receive it.
    "I am!" Claim it.
    Therefore, Gemstone, it's so.

JUNE 14 GEM
Gullibility.

So, you're just going to keep falling for the same "okey-doke"?

Really?

You know their explanation is a bunch of crap.

With your own eyes and ears, you see and hear exactly what's going on, but you allow and accept recreated versions of the truth.

Are you that weak-minded?

At this point, you are to blame, too, for always falling for messes so easily—the credulity of it all!

Stop being so *gullible!* You are not five years old anymore. You know how to put two and two together concerning the people you keep company with, people who have proven themselves to be deceptive towards you and others.

Gemstone, you are a grown woman! Snap out of being so "green" unless you're okay with entertaining the devil you know...who then opens the door and invites in the devils you don't.

JUNE 15 GEM
Past, present, and future.

"If you are depressed, you are living in the past; if you are anxious, you are living in the future; and if you are at peace, you are living in the present."
—Lau Tzu, the great Chinese philosopher

Being in a state of depression will keep you tied to past events or situations that will in turn keep you in a state of discontent and sorrow.

Feeling anxious is tied to what's to come or what may never come, resulting in uncontrollable fear, worry, and doubt.

Being at peace is the perfect state to be in. You're not concerned with the past, nor are you worried about the future. You're mindful and living in the now and experiencing good vibrations and frequencies.

May peace be unto you, Gemstone.

JUNE 16 GEM
Plot twist.

- ✓ You're not the failure they said you would be.
- ✓ You're not undesirable like they said you were.
- ✓ You're not the mean person they declared you to be.
- ✓ You're not weak minded like they said you were.
- ✓ You're not irresponsible like they labeled you to be.
- ✓ You're not a mistake like they said you were.
- ✓ You're not the lonely person you thought you would be.
- ✓ You're not a "waste of matter" like they said you were.
- ✓ You're not the uneducated woman they claimed you to be.
- ✓ You're not useless like they said you were.
- ✓ You're not the people pleaser they depended on you to be.
- ✓ You're not incompetent like they said you were.
- ✓ You're not heartless like they accused you to be.
- ✓ You're not fake and phony like they said you were.
- ✓ You're not lacking substance like they claimed you to be.
- ✓ You're not a generational failure like they said you were.

Plot twist—you won in life, Gemstone!—Because you're everything and far beyond what they ever thought you could or would be.

JUNE 17 GEM
Free your mind.

What issues do you continuously hold onto that are disturbing your peace and disrupting you from making big moves in life?

Rid your mind of incessant thoughts that mentally block you from doing what you need to do to be successful to "Secure the bag!" Remember, the mind controls the body, so whatever you're thinking affects the body and determines what moves you make.

You must forgive people! Learn Emotional Freedom Techniques (EFT) to bring people-pleasing and approval-seeking behaviors to an end and envision yourself as the person you desire to be. You can *free your mind* by decluttering your stuff to remove distractions, by releasing your regrets, and by becoming a forever learner according to life coach, Jennifer Smith in her 2022 *Lifehack* article, "30 Simple Ways to Free Your Mind Immediately."

Gemstone, if you severely struggle with *freeing your mind* or if your issues are deep-seated, the best solution is to seek professional help.

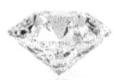

JUNE 18 GEM

They don't always love you back.

Gemstone, sometimes the people you love *don't always love you back.*

It may be no fault of your own, because some people don't even love themselves.

Again, it may be no fault of your own, <u>because some people don't even love themselves.</u>

JUNE 19 GEM
For the culture.

Cultures speak to the beliefs, values, foods, languages, practices, technologies, clothing, and styles of different groups of people all around the world.

What are you doing *for the culture*? Are you stepping out of the box and trying new experiences that add value to yourself and to your culture?

What new foods have you tasted? What new wines have you sipped, what new places have you traveled to, what new hairstyles have you worn, what new clothing trends have you tried that speak to your culture?

Embrace new adventures!

Visit Mayan caves in Mexico, not just the resort poolside bars. Climb the Diamond Head volcanic cone in Hawaii or experience an authentic luau and eat pineapples, poi, and saimin. Surf on Waikiki beach and do things beyond just wearing an artificial lei.

In Jamaica, try the authentic jerk dishes, Blue Mountain coffee, and ginger beer. Visit the historic Dunn's River Falls and listen to live reggae music. Go beyond putting your toes in the sand!

Partake in private boat tours in Positano and the Amalfi Coast in Italy. Hike the Path of the Gods, sip Italy's famous limoncello, and devour its *gnocchi alla sorrentina* and *insalata caprese*.

Tap into what culture is and what culture is about

to become a more well-rounded person. You'll come to appreciate even more just how different the world is.

Do it *for the culture,* Gemstone!

JUNE 20 GEM

Pause.

If your energy is off and you're doing too much, it's time to *pause*.

If your mouth is reckless, your actions are questionable, and you're being unreasonable, it's time to *pause*.

When you're "out of pocket" or your equilibrium is off, you need to *pause* and recollect yourself, because that type of behavior does not represent you well, nor does it respect the people around you who may experience secondhand embarrassment from your conduct.

Gemstone, listen to your inner voice when it tells you "Sit this one out."

Taking a *pause* is just resetting—it allows you to self-evaluate and pinpoint the underlying issue of your feelings and behavior so that you can properly address what's really going on.

JUNE 21 GEM
Give credit and support.

Have you ever noticed how people have a tendency to not to give credit to others when they clearly deserve it?

You helped another person complete a project at work...and then suddenly your name is not on the final report.

You helped someone...and when they succeeded, they never said "Thank you."

You supported someone significantly...but when they were promoted, they forgot all about you.

When it comes to gender, women do this to other women more often than they do it to men, and there's research to back this! According to Dr. Shawn Andrews' article "Why Women Don't Always Support Other Women" that ran in *Forbes* in January 2020, there are many reasons why women do not support or give credit to other women, among them the "power dead-even rule."

Defy that rule and *give credit and support,* Gemstone! Be part of making more room at the table for *all* women. Stop icing out other women, especially when they have played a significant role in your success.

JUNE 22 GEM
Highs and lows.

You don't have to take over the world today—it's okay to do the bare minimum just to get by.

Every day isn't always going to be rosy, because gloomy days somehow find their way to fit in between the good ones.

There will be highs and there will be lows. Gemstone, aim for the highs but still be content when you hit a few lows. Of course, the highs tend to go by very quickly while the lows can feel long and dreadful.

Own the version that your day turns out to be and try as much as possible to make the best of it. Tomorrow you'll have another chance to take over the world.

JUNE 23 GEM
Get back fine.

Okay, Gemstone, so you let yourself go. Life came at you fast and unfortunately keeping yourself up took a back seat, but today is the day you start owning your appearance.

Quickly start *getting back fine* by:

- ✓ Exercising regularly
- ✓ Eating right
- ✓ Applying moisturizing products or oils daily that smooth your skin
- ✓ Fixing your hair and makeup in a new way
- ✓ Looking your best from head to toe (i.e., wearing fitted clothes)
- ✓ Wearing the biggest smile
- ✓ Being responsible for owning your day

JUNE 24 GEM

Talk to strangers.

As a child, you were conditioned to not *talk to strangers* for the mere fact that they could be untrustworthy and dangerous.

But now that you're an adult, you can use your good judgment and sensibly engage unfamiliar people in conversation, people who are outside of your circle.

Gemstone, sensibly *talking to strangers* is a great way to "know what you don't know."

Connect with people who are the polar opposite of you to learn and grow and to be exposed to new theories, concepts, solutions, books, processes, documentaries, expanded networks, and friends. That's how you gain new perspectives!

JUNE 25 GEM
Your physical characteristics.

Your moles, freckles, dimples, small lips, big lips, wide hips, big toes, tiny toes, big feet, little feet, streaks of gray hair, red hair, blue eyes, brown eyes, big nose, pinched nose, small ears, big ears, tiny booty, big booty, birthmark, thick eyebrows, no eyebrows, itty-bitty chest, double-Ds, short neck, long neck, large knuckles, tall stature, mini stature, knock knees, thin hair, thick hair, short hair, long hair, large hands, tiny hands, skinny legs, thick thighs, almond-shaped eyes, downturned eyes, petite frame, large frame, and whatever else that stands out about you is what gives you character.

Your physical characteristics distinguish you and make you different from everyone else. You're special and unique because your Maker made no mistakes in making you.

What you may see as an image flaw is truly your incredible and distinctive physical character.

Gemstone, you are truly a natural beauty.

JUNE 26 GEM

Don't worry about tomorrow.

Tomorrow will take care of itself.

Worrying does not add a single hour, day, or moment to your life (Matt. 6:27, Luke 12:25).

Gemstone, focus on today—that time right in front of you. It's quite a special day since you'll only experience it once and only for a grand total of 24 hours.

Remember, every day is special! Tomorrow will be here soon enough.

JUNE 27 GEM
"Take me out the group chat!"

It's the constant notifications, the untimely and annoying dings, the excessive pictures, videos, and link sharing, the nonstop phone vibrations throughout the night, the late responders, the crack-of-dawn texters, the inside jokes, the silent readers-yet-nonresponders, the dissertation texters, the unknown numbers, the off-topic conversations, the corny memes, the annoying LOLs, the two individuals who refuse to sidebar their exchanges, the extreme braggers, the endless buy-my-products and donate-to-this requesters, the screaming-with-all-caps texters, the group thread's admin taking their role way too seriously, the "you haven't responded yet" reminders, the text ignorers, the "no one's safe" arguments, the annoying hashtags, the "that was my kid" texter who responded to the group texters, and more.

Gemstone, be thankful for the Mute, Block Sender, and Leave Group features. All of these help protect your mental health.

Though sometimes you just have to say, *"Take me out the group chat!"*

JUNE 28 GEM
Looks good on you.

- ✓ Keep at it.
- ✓ Keep pushing the envelope.
- ✓ Keep your foot on the gas.
- ✓ Keep zeroing in.
- ✓ Keep giving it your all.
- ✓ Keep them talking.
- ✓ "Keep your foot on their necks."
- ✓ Keep pushing forward.
- ✓ Keep applying pressure.
- ✓ Keep them guessing.
- ✓ Keep improving.
- ✓ Keep advancing.

Gemstone, keep at it, because progress *looks good on you.*

JUNE 29 GEM
Live a little.

You work hard every day; you've been constantly grinding and in full execution mode. So while you're out "G.I.-Jane'n" the world, don't forget to *live a little*.

Gemstone, take a few days to reset and recharge! *Live a little*, do the things you enjoy doing the most, and then get back in the game.

Your body will always thank you.

JUNE 30 GEM
Face your fear.

Fear is *false evidence appearing real.*

Sometimes the frightening thoughts in your head can feel so real, but that's just it—it's all in your head. Stop fearing things, because a lot of the things people worry about never even come to fruition.

According to Dr. Don Joseph Goewey, studies reveal that the majority of the things you worry about—85%, to be exact—never even happen, but your obsessive thoughts allow what you fear to constantly play out in your mind as if it's going to happen. This causes you unnecessary anxiety.

In the long run, if you fail to replace these fearful negative thoughts with positive ones, you can fall victim to manifesting your own misfortunes. Why? Because your mind is so powerful that it controls how you approach and react to things.

Stop allowing negative thoughts, people, and things to scare and worry you. Most of the time, what you fear is not even real. If it is, *face your fear* to overcome it.

Gemstone, you are designed to face anything life throws your way! That's what causes you to grow as a person. So many great success and survival stories prove this.

So, face your fear.

JULY 1 GEM
Intimacy.

How well do you and your significant other see into each other?

Gemstone, are you comfortable letting your defenses down and being vulnerable with your mate?

Intimacy is about seeing someone beyond the surface level and diving deep behind what they represent externally in order to truly know the ins and outs of who they are.

Intimacy = in-to-me-see.

A high level of trust is needed between you and your partner to feel comfortable and safe and able to connect on a very personal level.

Where trust does not exist, neither should *intimacy*.

JULY 2 GEM
Living rent-free.

Do you hold grudges from past situations that are over and done?

Did a person upset you and then went on their merry way...but that person nonetheless continues to occupy your thoughts? Are you agitated about things of the past that are petty in the grand scheme of things?

If you answered "yes" to any of these questions, then these people and things are *living rent-free* in your head.

Gemstone, your obsession over insignificant people whom you allow to kick back on a cheap futon in your head is ridiculous and unproductive. They're continuing to *live rent-free* in your head because you feel they didn't experience any repercussions.

What was said or done can't be changed or undone. Constantly thinking about it is not worth your time. It's time to let it go!

Replace such neurotic and endless thoughts with your hopes and dreams, because the rent in your headspace should never be free.

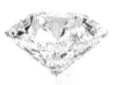

JULY 3 GEM
It's far beyond.

Your ability to create *is far beyond* what you believe—
you just have to unlock the other 90% of your brain that
some neuroscientists say most people don't even use.

Gemstone, the key to unlocking your brain is boosting your memory, focus, and mental skills.

To go further with your capabilities to create, engage
all of your senses! Learn new skills and build your vocabulary. Boost that brain!

JULY 4 GEM
Assume it.

Get in the habit of assuming that you already have the qualities you desire even if you're not 100% sure you already possess them at the moment.

Instill in yourself a reputation to live up to...and then do your best to live up to it!

Infuse yourself with confidence by repeating "I am" affirmations daily (refer to the January 31st Gem).

Gemstone, you may not have it all together right now, but believing, practicing, and generating self-esteem while legitimately acquiring your desired skill set will help positively change your own attitudes and perceptions of yourself as well as how others perceive you.

JULY 5 GEM
Once you know...

Gemstone, once you gain new knowledge or information or learn how to do something, you become responsible for what you do with it.

When you were a child and were learning right from wrong, your parents held you accountable for what you knew, from washing your hands before you ate to not chewing gum in bed and not taking your sibling's toys without first asking.

Responsibility begins at a tender age and carries into adulthood.

Sadly, some adults choose not to acquire knowledge and information as a way to shield themselves from responsibility.

Be responsible for what you know! For adults, ignorance is not bliss—it's just being irresponsible.

JULY 6 GEM
"This too shall pass."

Life's happenstances can tend to make you feel that the way things are now will always be the way they are, but as the adage goes, the truth is that *"this too shall pass."*

The hurt, pain, and sorrow you may be experiencing at a given time will eventually subside.

Gemstone, you'll get through whatever you're going through and you will be okay.

Remember that *"this too shall pass"*...as long as you allow it to.

JULY 7 GEM
Morning motivation.

Establish a personal motivational routine for when your feet hit the ground every morning.

Get yourself pumped up with high energy! Know that you are going to conquer the day! Download a morning "inspo" app on your phone to give you the quote of the day, jam out to your favorite inspirational songs, read daily devotions to help stimulate positive thinking, even give yourself a high five in your mirror to stop self-criticism from taking charge of your day. That last habit is recommended by Mel Robbins, author of *The High 5 Habit.*

Morning motivational routines will help trigger your inner winning spirit and give you the boost you need to not only start your day but to dominate it. Gemstone, your daily *morning motivational routine* reinforces the positive thoughts that are already embedded within you, thoughts like "I can do this!" "I'm a winner!" "I got this!" "I'm amazing!" "I'm a boss!" "Don't quit!" "Get it, girl!" "Yaaasss, Queen!" and so many more. All of these will solidify your inner greatness.

Wake up each day courageously expressing how you plan to be your best! And know that what you plan to accomplish today will put you one step closer to "securing the bag" and achieving your goals.

JULY 8 GEM

Ask for forgiveness.

Asking for forgiveness goes a lot further than just saying "I'm sorry."

Forgiveness is requesting that the other party will not hold whatever was done to them against you, while just saying "sorry" can be impersonal and broader in terms of what it really means.

Gemstone, make your apology personable and meaningful by asking for compassion, reconciliation, mercy, and tolerance. All of those are bundled into the word "forgiveness."

JULY 9 GEM
Finish unfinished business.

Don't allow unresolved situations to linger.

Avoid continuing to repress your emotions and memories surrounding an experience that you need to come to terms with.

Having a conversation with those involved may no longer be warranted, but you need to process your feelings fully and settle on a conclusion and closure.

Deal with what's not been dealt with. Don't allow unfinished business to fester and become an emotional disease.

Gemstone, seek professional help or group therapy if you're struggling with *finishing unfinished business.*

JULY 10 GEM
What happens?

Gemstone, you have major goals and dreams in life, but achieving them always seems to be derailed by time, resources, and most of all, fear.

Say you want to start a YouTube movie review channel but are scared that viewers will not like your channel. Besides, you know that competition for viewers on YouTube is quite fierce.

What happens if you don't start your channel?

Not starting your channel means you won't get to put out your content. Then viewers will never get to decide if they like your channel...which eliminates opportunities to get viewer subscriptions. Then you won't have to worry about any criticisms because you won't have an audience to criticize you...but you can also forget about any forms of monetization or ad revenue.

What happens if you do start your channel?

Starting your channel means you'll get to put tons of content out there, allow viewers to review your channel, and receive viewer feedback through likes, comments, and subscriptions. Starting your channel means you'll be able to ask viewers for movies they'd like you to review. It also means you'll receive more inspiration from your audience to expand your content and that you can use audience criticism to improve your channel...and then potentially gain endless opportunities to grow your channel and network to gain monetization opportunities, ad revenue, brand partnerships, and more.

Asking yourself *what happens* if you do and *what happens* if you don't helps you see that pushing past your excuses and pursuing your goals and dreams outweighs all the reasons not to.

JULY 11 GEM
No more defending.

Stop going through hell and high water to defend yourself from people who are unwilling to accept your truth.

It's clear that they do not understand you, nor do they believe you.

The false allegations they made against you are preposterous and are soaking up your energy. This is not a friendship! It is also not a relationship worth salvaging. Exhausting is what it is.

Gemstone, stop falling into the vicious cycle of defending your character and values to someone who does not respect them, someone who holds you to a different standard than others.

Bring to a hard stop the cycle of defending yourself when you've done nothing wrong.

JULY 12 GEM
Don't accept applications or invitations.

Gemstone, you have a game plan that you promised yourself you would stick to.

This game plan requires you to make some serious sacrifices up front regarding how you use your time in order to accomplish your goals.

Therefore, *do not accept applications or invitations* for new acquaintances, tasks, projects, brunches, dinners, organizations, clubs, outings, or anything else that sidetracks you from getting the ball rolling.

This may seem harsh, but it's only temporary and it's how real CEOs, leaders, and trendsetters operate—they *stop accepting applications and invitations* to protect their time so that they can achieve their goals.

This is a guaranteed way to stay committed to your game plan.

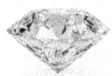

JULY 13 GEM
Sangria for the soul.

Doctoring up your wine with fruit, juice, carbonated water, and more makes for quite a refreshing drink after a long day of work.

Thanks to the Spaniards, a glass of refreshing sangria can liven up your day.

One can only think how well the Spaniards studied Psalm 104:15.

Salud, Gemstone!

JULY 14 GEM
A consumption tank of information.

Every day you spent in grade school and then in college, grad, or trade school, you were committed to learning, studying, and growing. But once you graduated, you may have stopped doing those things and instead transitioned to just doing the normal and daily activities that your career requires.

Gemstone, you should never stop learning and growing. You should never stop feeding and filling your brain with knowledge.

To remain competitive and marketable, to have elevated business savvy and strategic skills, allow your mind to continue to be a *consumption tank of information.*

To do this, keep reading, enroll in courses, and study relevant literature and business publications.

There are so many valuable sources of information and continuing education! Examples include college lectures on an array of topics and theories that you can access online from professors at major universities such as Duke, Yale, Harvard, and Illinois State. Also look for such lectures on Audible and YouTube and directly on *The Great Courses* website.

JULY 15 GEM
Your dash.

The years between the day you were born and the day your life's journey in the land of the living is called to an end are *your dash*.

Make *your dash* count, Gemstone.

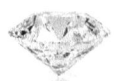

JULY 16 GEM
Defense mechanisms.

What behavior do you automatically project when you're trying to immediately disassociate yourself from something?

Is it repression, denial, projection, displacement, or regression? Is it sublimation, distortion, intellectualization, assertiveness, rationalization, undoing, or compensation?

Whatever your *defense mechanism* is, you unconsciously use it to protect yourself from potential anxiety.

Gemstone, the best way to stop your *defense mechanisms* is to actually experience the emotion you feel in the moment versus allowing your *defense mechanism* reaction to take over for you.

JULY 17 GEM
Perhaps.

Perhaps what they are saying about you is true.

Are you mature enough to self-evaluate and determine the validity of someone else's characterization of you? Surely everyone can't be lying or creating falsehoods about you 100% of the time.

What stands out about your character that needs some work? What can you own about yourself and commit to improving?

Today is a great day to start working on whatever that is, Gemstone.

JULY 18 GEM
Disclaimers.

Are you constantly having to make a *disclaimer* before sharing a message when conversing with friends?

If you are, then you know that what you're sharing with them more than likely bothers them in some kind of way. If it didn't, why would you need to precede your conversations and messages with pretenses?

Here's the thing: real friends don't always need *disclaimers* because they know and accept you for who you are.

Evaluate the reasons you excessively give *disclaimers*. Is it because your friends are super sensitive or because they are super judgy?

Gemstone, know who you can and can't let your hair down with.

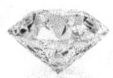

JULY 19 GEM
Assume positive intent.

Gemstone, everyone is not always mean, sneaky, or conniving.

Could their critical feedback really have been meant to lift you up versus put you down?

Was beginning the project a week earlier without you more about them trying to get things moving along to meet the deadline—after all, you were busy—or was it about them trying to receive all the credit?

Was ordering your dinner before you arrived a nice gesture—then your order could be placed before the restaurant's rush happened—or was it them being controlling?

Assuming positive intent will bring your defenses down and help you start thinking differently based on the idea that people are for you and not against you.

Though this can be a much harder mindset to adopt nowadays, leading with the idea that people genuinely mean well and are trying their best sets the stage for developing better relationships personally and professionally.

JULY 20 GEM
Be wild at heart.

That adventurous spirit in you must live!

Be like the illustrious mustang—cultivate strong survival instincts, feel out your environment for its sustainability, and communicate with your herd (i.e., the ones closest to you) to receive guidance and muster up appropriate and quick responses to life's challenges.

Gemstone, remember to love unconditionally, be passionate about your life, and remove all restraints.

Be wild at heart.

JULY 21 GEM

Create the ambiance that you desire.

Gemstone, *create the ambiance that you desire* from where you are today.

Don't wait until you sail over the Mediterranean seas to enjoy your ideal ambience! Create a living space filled with cherished details and designs and romantic aesthetics now.

Creating the atmosphere and the feeling of a place where you want to be will set your mind at ease and give you a peaceful experience within your very own humble abode.

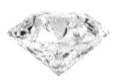

JULY 22 GEM
Hindsight is 20/20.

When critical issues and emergencies arise, get through those first.

Solve what needs to be solved right away and then seek to fully understand the whys and hows *after* you've dealt with the situation.

It's easier and clearer to comprehend the reason why something happened after it has happened and it's a settled matter versus when you're going through it.

The mind processes better when it's outside of a given problem. That's why it's more challenging to make sense of situations while you're still in the midst of them.

Hindsight is 20/20, Gemstone, because deep reflection and review have had a chance to occur. After the situation is when you can look back and understand how and where things could've gone differently...and usually much better.

JULY 23 GEM
Identify what holds you back.

So you're fully engaged in accomplishing your goals, but every time you reach a certain point, you cave in and completely give up.

It never fails—you stop at that very specific point every single time. Why? Because there's something about that part of the process that you feel disconnected from, uncomfortable with, hate doing, or lack the knowledge or expertise to do.

Identify the exact part of the process that holds you back and seek the help of someone who's skilled in that aspect to do it. Ask them for guidance or hire them to do it for you, because you don't have time to keep starting over. Getting their assistance will be worth it!

Did you write the book but didn't publish it because you aren't good at editing? Hire an editor.

Did you purchase the domain name but never built the website? Hire a website designer.

Did you write scripts for your "How To" series of YouTube videos but never recorded any of them? Hire a videographer.

Get the help and support you need, Gemstone, for that one thing. Then you can forge ahead with accomplishing your goals.

JULY 24 GEM
Preferences.

You are entitled to your own *preferences.*

Don't allow anyone to tell you otherwise.

You are attracted to what you're attracted to, you like what you like, you despise what you despise, you love what you love.

Your *preferences* are your *preferences,* and those are simply what you prefer, Gemstone.

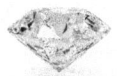

JULY 25 GEM
Not my problem.

Disable your phone's voicemail.

When the same people continue to call you with their dilemmas, issues, crises, and other activities that constantly steer you away from the things you need to do or your personal goals, do not pick up the phone.

Let them receive the message from your phone company that says, "I'm sorry, but the person you are trying to reach has a voicemail box that has not been set up yet. Goodbye."

This technique transfers their issues back onto them versus them waiting for you to call back with a solution. In essence, not answering your phone teaches people to stop depending on you and blaming you when their issues are not resolved because you didn't return their call after they left you a voicemail about their dilemma.

The same goes for text messages—set your text messages to auto-respond to let people know that you are not receiving texts at this time.

Gemstone, these features are built into your phone for a reason! Use them.

Grown adults need to stop making you the solution to their problems when they face issues like needing to borrow money, complete tasks, and do anything else that—if they weren't expecting you to take over—would allow them to go through a process of their own that would help them develop as people and give them the life skills they need to be successful.

Decide if disabling your voicemail and blocking your text messages temporarily would give you peace of mind and force others to become more responsible for handling their own problems. Which is a form of tough love.

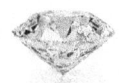

JULY 26 GEM
Lip service.

It's better to show them than tell them.

Telling your mate that you love them but not showing them that through your actions is just *lip service.*

You can have the "gift of the gab" and speak eloquently and metaphorically about how much you love someone, but the real value and meaning of those words lie in showing them how you feel.

Putting love into action, Gemstone, is a daily commitment.

In action, love looks like warm hugs, kisses, encouragement, kind words, support, intimacy, your time, consoling, forgiveness, showing up, being there, and sacrificing.

JULY 27 GEM
Look in the mirror.

Take a long *look in the mirror* and stare yourself up and down.

Hopefully you like what you see.

If you don't like what you see, then the image of the woman you desire to be will be reflected in the back of your mind versus in the mirror in front of you.

You can become the woman you want to be, but you must do the work.

Are you willing to put in the work, Gemstone? Are you willing to make the changes and the sacrifices you absolutely need to make in order to become the woman you desire to be?

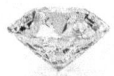

JULY 28 GEM
Successful leadership.

Gemstone, becoming a *successful leader* is no longer about you, but about the team you lead and your commitment to that team.

10 pillars of leadership:

1. Build relationships and trust with each team member and engage with them regularly.
2. Ensure that you know what each team member brings to the table and that they are in the right position.
3. Share your story and career journey and sense of life with the team and allow them to see the value you bring as the leader every day.
4. Keep the team well-informed and help them see the bigger picture by reminding them of the importance of each of their roles.
5. Manage problems effectively and remove troublemakers.
6. Reward your team and reward them often.
7. Use persuasion with your team versus intimidation.
8. Protect your team from outsiders and negativity.
9. Trust and verify your team's work.
10. Coach and provide feedback to all members of your team frequently.

JULY 29 GEM
The sky is the limit!

You've heard that phrase before, but it's only true when you truly believe it.

Gemstone, if you believe that your possibilities are limited, then your thinking is capped and your ability to increase who and what you are and your levels of self-development will peak at the limits that your mind has imposed on you.

Let *the sky be your limit!* Then your maximum potential is uncapped.

JULY 30 GEM
Avoid superficial behavior.

Are you concerned only with the obvious—their good looks, smile, and physique?

Do you avoid the depth or context or character of a person because they are just so mesmerizing to you?

If you do, that's *superficial behavior.*

Gemstone, snap into reality! Go beyond the surface level, a.k.a. their "representative." Learn the ins and outs of a person to see if this is truly a good pairing for you to pursue.

JULY 31 GEM
Get help.

Gemstone, you are not an octopus with eight hands, nor are you designed to do everything. It's better to pay for services and thus have time given back to you. As Benjamin Franklin said, "Time is money."

In finance, the time value of money (TVM) concept tells us the same thing: time is money and time is very valuable now, while you have it.

You are a busy person because you have real goals to achieve in life. Therefore, make the most out of your day by pursuing convenient solutions when others offer to help. It's worth your time and your money!

Today's conveniences:

- ✓ Grocery delivery: Instacart, Amazon Fresh
- ✓ Online shopping: Amazon, Overstock, Target
- ✓ Food delivery: Uber Eats, Door Dash, Postmates, Grubhub
- ✓ Online car shopping and delivery: Carvana, Vroom
- ✓ Home cleaning services: Merry Maids, Molly Maid
- ✓ Virtual personal assistants: Time Etc., MyTasker, BELAY
- ✓ Online notary services: Notarize.com, NotaryLive

AUGUST 1 GEM
Queens seek council.

As early as 3000 BC, when monarchies and kingdoms existed, kings and queens who sat on the throne had councils.

The King's Council or Queen's Council was composed of a selected group of advocates and advisors who provided the king or queen with the wisdom and guidance they needed to rule their kingdom.

Gemstone, being the queen that you are, who's sitting on your council? Who have you selected to advocate for you and advise you?

Ensure that you have strong counsel in your life, because success lies within counsel (Prov. 11:14, 15:22).

AUGUST 2 GEM
From your lips to God's ears.

The Arabic and Hebraic adage *"From your lips to God's ears"* is a reminder to wish, dream, hope, and believe aloud to the one above, because your request will be heard.

The strong connection between *your lips and God's ears* is that your lips must speak exactly what you want and God's ears will hear you.

Prayer is considered the divine and most sacred way to ask for what you want and express confidently and boldly what you want to the one who "sits high and looks low" (Psa. 138:6).

So, Gemstone, take time today to make what your heart desires known unto your Higher Power. Verbally put your request into the atmosphere to give it life and to feel it in your soul.

The electromagnetic energy generated from your lips to God's ears creates a sacred frequency and vibration through sound waves, elevating your conscious and subconscious mind to be in the position to believe that you will receive exactly what you pray for.

AUGUST 3 GEM
Girls' night!

Yes, Gemstone, you need *girls' nights!*

"Turn up" with your girlfriends every once in a while.

Connect, relax, socialize, share, and have fun, because anything less is counterproductive to creating life's needed and memorable moments.

Mimosas up!

AUGUST 4 GEM
"I am what I say I am."

That timeless saying continues to prove itself over and over again.

"I am what I say I am" are words manifested by you, the person speaking them. We believe what we ourselves say we are more than what anyone else tells us we are.

Positive or negative, our beliefs can be significantly influenced by others, but what we believe and what we say to ourselves is our reality.

People can give you all the compliments in the world and keep telling you how great you are, but the only compliments that carry realness and certitude are the compliments you give yourself when you say how great you are.

Proclaim who you are confidently and boldly! You can do this by speaking aloud the daily affirmations shared in the January 31 Gem.

Gemstone, it's your job to manifest your greatness. Manifest it by speaking it and feed it by speaking it day and night!

AUGUST 5 GEM

No games!

Let your "yes" be "yes" and your "no" be "no."

Don't play games with people—just "come correct" with your intentions. Either "yes" you will or "no" you won't...and then stick to your decision.

Wishy-washy behavior is literally the one thing that many people cannot stand. Can you?

Gemstone, be clear and concise about what you do want to do and what you don't want to do and leave silly mind games to children.

AUGUST 6 GEM
Don't let them ruin it for you.

Are you allowing others to ruin things for you?

You're better than that! You love yourself and you have the power to either accept or reject people's negative interjections that grossly attempt to interfere with your happiness.

Gemstone, use your power to take back control of your narrative.

AUGUST 7 GEM

Under promise and overdeliver.

Never overpromise or overcommit to anything. Instead, state exactly what you can do and then do it.

Do not mislead people and get them excited for the "extra" you promised that you know you may not actually be able to deliver. Time and time again, overpromising and underdelivering has resulted in big flops and great losses of credibility.

Gemstone, it's better to *under promise and overdeliver.* Deliver more than what you committed to! That impresses every time.

AUGUST 8 GEM
The Tinder Swindler.

You've probably seen or heard about the 2022 Netflix documentary, *The Tinder Swindler*—it has taken over social media by storm.

Gemstone, this documentary is about a fraudster who lures women into relationships and then scams them for their money. Take that as a warning!

Never, ever give a man you're not married to/have a long-term commitment with or have legitimate business dealings with any amount of money.

A time may come when a man you love and care about finds himself in a real bind, but the best way to support him in challenging times is by giving him words of encouragement, praying for him, and directing him to other helpful resources.

If you do feel compelled to financially support him in a situation, then do so with a small and insignificant amount of funds that you're willing to part with permanently. Only you will know your limits and tolerance when it comes to extending financial support to someone facing a real emergency.

BUT! Importantly, if a man you are just getting to know is asking you for money, that is a red flag, because "the math is not mathing." Proceed with caution!

AUGUST 9 GEM

"But they're family!"

Gemstone, saying that someone is family is a terrible excuse for co-signing messy behavior.

You know that some of your relatives are toxic, foul-acting, out of line, and a bad influence on the person you are today.

The real question is this: would you associate yourself with them if they weren't your family?

If the answer is "no," then you have some decisions to make.

It may be time to start distancing yourself to protect your image, beliefs, values, reputation, and the respected person that you are.

AUGUST 10 GEM
Real leaders...

- ✓ Real leaders are influential.
- ✓ Real leaders are aspirational.
- ✓ Real leaders are inspirational.
- ✓ Real leaders are motivators.
- ✓ Real leaders are transformational.
- ✓ Real leaders care about their people.
- ✓ Real leaders encourage and reinforce change.
- ✓ Real leaders think strategically.
- ✓ Real leaders tie their goals to the goals of the organization.
- ✓ Real leaders develop their people.
- ✓ Real leaders correct and coach their people.
- ✓ Real leaders promote accountability.
- ✓ Real leaders thrive with team success.
- ✓ Real leaders are great listeners.
- ✓ Real leaders are great communicators.
- ✓ Real leaders groom others to become leaders.

Gemstone, are you a *real leader?*

AUGUST 11 GEM
Make it known.

Require respect from the get-go by *making it known* to others what your beliefs and values are.

Don't leave room for others to guess.

Gemstone, be up-front and firm about who you are and what you stand for...and what you will and will not tolerate.

AUGUST 12 GEM
Blessing jar.

A lovely ʻanakē ("auntie" in Hawaiian) gave her family beautifully crafted *blessing jars* one year for Christmas. Her instructions were to fill the jars throughout the year with jotted-down moments when each family member had received a blessing, big or small. Come the end of the year, they'd open their jars and count all of their blessings—which were so many—to help remind them of how blessed they were.

People often forget how blessed they are. They take so many things for granted, from waking up to having clothes to wear, food to eat, a family, friends, their jobs, a means of transportation, and a home to live in.

Make your own *blessings jar*, box, or mug—whatever works. Start jotting down your blessings and dropping them in the jar. Pull out a blessing when you're having a bad day or on the last day of the year to revisit your blessings and see how far you've come.

Always count your blessings, Gemstone, because they add up.

AUGUST 13 GEM
Sheer luck.

Is it *sheer luck* how far you've come in life, or could it be something more?

Gemstone, are you sure it wasn't your faith, discipline, dedication, and tenacity that has gotten you where you are?

Never discount the hard work you've put in to get this far in life.

AUGUST 14 GEM
Social responsibility.

Gemstone, look beyond caring just for yourself and think about how you can contribute to the welfare of society.

Social responsibility speaks to the ethical framework of how individuals, employers, and others can better their communities and environments.

Everything all the time can't be just me, me, me. What good is that? How selfish is that? How are you fulfilled by doing absolutely nothing to uplift the less fortunate? There are so many things you can do to contribute to the betterment of society!

Small gestures and efforts can be very impactful.

7 ways to be socially responsible:

1. Give gently used clothes to homeless shelters or city collection boxes.
2. Drop off nonperishable items at local food banks.
3. Donate to community organizations that directly help the less fortunate.
4. Hold community yard sales and give a percentage of the earnings to nonprofits.
5. Collect useful items and donations from local companies to distribute to the homeless.

6. Volunteer at local community farms to help plant healthy fruits and vegetables in areas with limited access to healthy foods.

7. Donate books and toys to orphanages and children's hospitals.

AUGUST 15 GEM
Extend a hand.

Did you have to put someone in their place or give them a piece of your mind? Tell them how foul-acting and concerning their behavior was? Lay them out for their grotesque actions?

Now it's time to simmer down.

After you've given them a good tongue-lashing, it's time to *extend a hand.*

Don't put someone down without *extending them a hand* up. Advise them on the best way to fix their situation and encourage them to do better.

"It's the Gemstone way!"

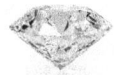

AUGUST 16 GEM
What people fear.

What people fear, they lie about.

This behavior starts at a very young age.

When children learn the difference between right and wrong and what the consequences of right and wrong actions are, some children begin to tell stories or lies when they feel like they might get in trouble for something they weren't supposed to do, like taking another cookie out of the jar or eating candy when they weren't supposed to or taking someone else's toys without asking. Whatever it is, they lie about what they did for fear of being scolded, losing their privileges, or being put in time-out.

Adults lie about what they're scared of or feel the need to protect. They lie about their real feelings to avoid having to be vulnerable. They lie about needing help to prevent others from mischaracterizing them. They lie and say that everything on the home front is okay when it's not to avoid conversations about their family issues and to protect themselves.

People fear what others think about them, they fear their personal business being spread, and they fear the potential outcomes of their shared information.

Gemstone, have a tight-knit circle of trusted friends or a confidante so that you have a safe space to be vulnerable, a space where you can receive guidance without any fears of judgment or false characterizations.

AUGUST 17 GEM
Make it fun.

You don't have to be super serious all the time.

Lighten up and find ways to make mundane and strenuous tasks fun! Reframe your "work" as being time challenges, milestone celebrations, competitions, and games.

Gemstone, you will be amazed at how much easier your work will become—and the incredible drive you will have—when you *make it fun.*

AUGUST 18 GEM
Workaholism.

Yes, it's a disease—it's the "ism" that gives it away.

Workaholics are addicted to their work. Nothing else matters to them. It is a compulsive behavior driven by the idea of achieving success, proving yourself, and needing to people-please.

Workaholism impacts your mental health because it's associated with extreme stress levels, depression, anxiety, and insomnia.

Gemstone, *workaholism* is a real thing! Seek the professional help you may need to get a proper diagnosis and to overcome your addiction to work.

AUGUST 19 GEM
Your weaknesses.

Gemstone, be careful with whom you share *your weaknesses.*

Unfortunately, there are people who will gladly use them against you. They will smile in your face but plot behind your back.

They may not be able to compete with you when it comes to your strengths, but they surely will try to hit you where you're weak and when you least expect it.

Protect your shortcomings, protect your flaws, protect your position.

AUGUST 20 GEM
Play the devil's advocate.

Highly intellectual people often express contentious opinions to challenge the strength of powerful arguments. Their pretending to be against the main argument stretches the thinking of others.

Playing devil's advocate is a clever way to draw out more reasoning and information to support the main argument for moving an idea forward. Leaders use this calculated strategy to prepare their team for handling harsh criticisms that may come at them from external sources.

Gemstone, if you *play devil's advocate*, you are promoting serious thinking among the collective.

Use this strategy to make yourself and others think and to increase your knowledge and understanding beyond your own perspective.

AUGUST 21 GEM
"I'll take peace of mind for $600, Alex."

Gemstone, congratulations—you hit a Jeopardy "Daily Double"!

Peace of mind is the absence of mental stress and anxiety.

Peace of mind comes with incomparable feelings of calmness, tranquility, and safety.

Peace of mind is having steadiness in life and being worry-free. Its value is intrinsic.

Seek peace.

AUGUST 22 GEM

The hardest person to forgive...

...is yourself.

Forgive yourself and do it often.

In life, the amount of guilt we feel after making mistakes or having done something deliberately is extremely heavy and feels unforgivable.

Some people find it hard to forgive themselves because of their culpability and feelings of inadequacy, but it's important to overcome guilt and shame.

Gemstone, you're always giving others second, third, and even fourth chances, so you must do the same for yourself.

The best way to forgive yourself is to write yourself a heartfelt apology. Read it aloud and ask yourself for forgiveness. Then give yourself forgiveness...and then let it go, because you are forgiven.

AUGUST 23 GEM
Pretty and petty.

The words *"pretty" and "petty"* are not synonymous.

Gemstone, it's always a good day to be pretty, but when your pettiness enters the room, the light no longer shines as brightly on what was so pretty about you.

Decide on how you want to show up today and every day.

Hope it's pretty!

AUGUST 24 GEM
POV.

Gemstone, seek to see both sides of the coin in all matters by looking at the whole picture first. This will prevent you from making hasty decisions.

Analyze both *points of view.* Just because you favor one person's *POV* more does not mean that the other person's information is less credible or that it's ineffective.

The details and information from both *POVs* will be vital for making the right choice. Therefore, stop limiting your own *POV* by limiting yourself to just one perspective.

Take the time to fully hear both sides! Use your critical thinking skills by always weighing opposing information before making any decisions.

AUGUST 25 GEM
Lashing out.

Do you allow anger, disappointment, or pain to externalize themselves and become physical and potentially hurtful actions?

What got you to this point, Gemstone?

Sometimes there are legitimate reasons to *lash out*, yes, but do so privately. Punch pillows, kung fu kick the air, yell like a hyena, and scream "Bloody Mary!" behind closed doors without causing harm to yourself, your property, or anyone else. Remember, once you cross a certain line, your adult temper tantrum will be upgraded to "destructive."

Always practice restraint and self-control.

It's best to leave the *lashing-out* and rolling-on-the-floor fits to two-year-olds.

AUGUST 26 GEM
Get money twice.

The best way to double up your money is to not ask for it—instead, do what Pitbull says and "Ask for advice, *get money twice.*"

You can make more money by asking someone for sound guidance and following through on what they say, because the money you seek is not found in the value of the dollar given to you but rather in the advice shared with you.

Their advice—if good—is an investment into your ability to obtain solutions and income.

Today's dollar that's handed to you, Gemstone, as a quick solution is outvalued by the wisdom that a person imparts to you. That wisdom means now you're empowered with the know-how to handle future problems and create lucrative opportunities for yourself for a lifetime.

Remember, you *get money twice* when you ask for advice.

AUGUST 27 GEM
Drop some F-bombs.

Say it: "I am favored, I am focused, I am fearless, I am friendly, I am fun, I am not fake, I am fine, I am free, I am flourishing, and I am faithful."

Say more: "I am fascinating, I am fair, I am a forgiver, I am fruitful, I am a fighter, I am first, I am familial, I am fantastic, I am fabulous, and I am fulfilled."

Gemstone, let these *F-bombs* resonate with you.

AUGUST 28 GEM
"Be intentional."

The common catchphrase *"Be intentional"* carries a heavy weight, but what does it truly mean?

To *be intentional* is to be purposeful in whatever you do. The intentional moves you make should put you one step closer to achieving your goals.

Answer these 6 questions:

1. Did the extra 5 minutes you added to yesterday's workout help you achieve your target heart rate?
2. Did you start creating your brand right after you finished reading that marketing book and researching branding?
3. Did decluttering your space give you the clarity you needed to better focus on your goals?
4. Did watching that YouTube video increase your skill set?
5. Did talking to that friend on the phone for two hours give you the encouragement you needed to push through?
6. Did creating a vision board inspire you to dream bigger?

If you answered "yes" to any of these questions, you are *being intentional*. If you couldn't answer "yes" to any of them, you need to up your intentions, Gemstone!

AUGUST 29 GEM
Something green.

Nutritionists advise eating *something green* with every meal because that's one of the easiest ways to begin improving your health.

Green leafy foods such as spinach, kale, and broccoli load up your body with antioxidants, minerals, fiber, and vitamins that boost you internally and externally.

Add a green vegetable to your breakfast, lunch, and dinner to reduce your chances of disease, obesity, and mental declination.

Remember, Gemstone, "health is wealth."

AUGUST 30 GEM

Reasons.

People only do things for three *reasons:* a good *reason,* a bad *reason,* and the real *reason.*

Gemstone, what's your *reason?*

AUGUST 31 GEM
Mess-ups.

Gemstone, normalize taking ownership of your own culpability and wrongdoings in life.

The more you try to make excuses for your own *mess-
ups*, the more you'll continue to stunt your growth and
your relationships with other people.

There is so much power in owning your "ish"! Owning
your *mess-ups* connects you to your integrity and your
humanity.

If you can't acknowledge your shortcomings from
within, then any apology you render will be disingenu-
ous, so forgive yourself first and then apologize for your
actions.

You don't have to go down into the deep depths of your
soul every time, but be simple and clear—say "I *messed
up*, and I apologize" and then share how you plan to
conduct yourself differently in the future.

This is you taking accountability for your bad behavior and the negative role you played in a situation.

Owning your *mess-ups* is an effective way to grow and
maintain your dignity and cultivate respect for yourself
and others.

SEPTEMBER 1 GEM
No desire to escape.

Do you find yourself always looking for something new—a new job, a new place to live, new friends, a new relationship, new hobbies, a new means of transportation?

If you're always seeking the new, then Gemstone, maybe it's time to set up a life that you don't need to escape from.

SEPTEMBER 2 GEM
Unmet expectations.

No matter whether you believe they're tapped into their "third eye" or not, people are not mind readers.

Gemstone, you must make known in your relationship exactly what you want. Clearly communicate your expectations and do not sugarcoat your desires. Be crisp, clear, and precise.

Particularly when it comes to marriage, do not allow *unmet expectations* to be your story—that's one of the top reasons why couples divorce, and it happens because one or both parties never communicated to their spouse their wants and needs. Don't let that be you; don't expect other people to be mind readers.

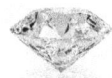

SEPTEMBER 3 GEM
Who are you?

You are so caught up with your title that you don't even know who you are.

But your executive or professional title is not who you are—it is what you do.

Being a mother, wife, friend, companion, and whatever else you call yourself is also not who you are—it's what you do.

Gemstone, who you are is comprised of your character, values, and beliefs. If you cannot define what your character, values, and beliefs are, then do you really know who you are?

When someone asks you who you are, remember to lead with your moral qualities, life principles, and beliefs before sharing all the "hats" you wear.

SEPTEMBER 4 GEM
Discretionary income.

Gemstone, have *discretionary income.*

Discretionary income or *DI* is the remaining money you have left to spend however you please after you've satisfied your financial obligations, including the money you've allocated for giving and saving.

Use your *DI* to enjoy yourself.

Go out to eat, go to the spa, go to a concert, go to the event...because what good is having *DI* if you never use it?

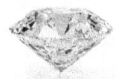

SEPTEMBER 5 GEM
Life skills.

Sad to say, not all women have mastered or are even aware of all of the *life skills* they need to run their household or just to have for their daily survival.

The simple way to fix this is to purchase a *life skills* book or reference an online checklist that provides a list of all the basics.

Some *life skills* that many women have not quite mastered:

- ✓ Changing a tire.
- ✓ Using a fire extinguisher.
- ✓ Unclogging a drain.
- ✓ Following a budget.
- ✓ Dripping pipes in a freeze.
- ✓ Changing air filters.
- ✓ Mowing a lawn.
- ✓ Filing important documents securely.
- ✓ Traveling internationally.
- ✓ Creating a basic will.

Gemstone, if you or someone you know hasn't mastered these *life skills*, get your hands on a simple *life skills* book, stat!

SEPTEMBER 6 GEM
Leave an account.

Your personal experiences deserve to be shared and left for those you wish to inspire and help and for those who are interested in your story.

Every Gemstone has a story to tell.

Document some of the most incredible, critical, and memorable moments of your life in an autobiography or memoir.

Your life is unforgettable! It is worthy of being captured and told in your own words.

Leave an account of the ebbs and flows of your life so that your loved ones can be inspired and have something to look up to and treasure.

SEPTEMBER 7 GEM

Give them their flowers now.

Celebrate people today! Right now!

Don't wait until the years have gone by and so many moments have passed. Don't wait until someone is elderly to celebrate them.

Give them their flowers now and let them know how much you appreciate and love them. Tell them how they've been such a great example for you to look up to or how they've been such an instrumental person in your life.

Gemstone, if unexpected world events and crises have shown you one thing, it's undoubtedly this: tomorrow is not promised.

Don't wait to give people their flowers when they're long gone—*give those flowers to them now*, while they can smell them.

SEPTEMBER 8 GEM
Chin up.

In the darkest hour, when you're at your lowest, the only place left to go is up.

Gemstone, keep your head lifted! People have been known to learn and grow when they've faced the hardest and most difficult challenges of their lives.

Coming out on the other side, you can look back and say it did you good to have gone through hardships, suffering, and misfortunes. Times like those show you what you're made of—they define your character more and more each time you go through them.

You're a gem! You're hard to cut, hard to scratch, and hard to break. You'll come out stronger, wiser, braver, happier, more well-rounded, more humbled. You'll be better.

Therefore, *chin up!* Always.

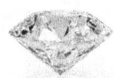

SEPTEMBER 9 GEM
See the splendor.

It takes tedious hand and wrist work to squeeze the juice out of lemons, but when the pitcher is finally filled and the sugar and ice are added, oh, how divine and refreshing the lemonade tastes!

When women go through the overwhelming and sometimes traumatic experience of giving birth, once the mother is holding her beautiful newborn baby, all the aches and pains she endured during the labor process are forgotten as she focuses on the bundle of joy in her arms.

Athletes preparing for championships go through seasons and years of practice and brutal training, but when they cross that finish line and are standing on the podium with their medals, they're no longer thinking about the arduous process it took to get there—they're thinking about their victory.

The process you must go through is not always joyous, but the other side is glorious.

Gemstone, push through your challenges to *see the splendor* on the other side.

SEPTEMBER 10 GEM
10,000 steps.

Pick up your feet and go! Walk, run, skip, hop, and jump.

10,000 steps are what's recommended as the minimum amount of movement you should do every day to have a healthy heart and healthy circulation and to stay fit.

Gemstone, excuses for why you don't yet have a healthier you are no longer excusable!

You can find thousands of videos on YouTube that will show you how to achieve your *10,000 daily steps* even in the confines of your own home.

Use your cell phone's fitness app to track your steps or purchase a fitness tracking device or pedometer to help you keep count.

Take note, that the level of where you want to go and be in life will only be able to go to the level that your body can take it—So get your steps in!

SEPTEMBER 11 GEM

Your own space.

In your home that you share with others—a spouse, family members, roommates—you deserve some space of your own.

If your home is big, finding a quiet place to selah should not be a problem.

If your home is small, find your solace in your tub, in your closet, or somewhere that barricades you from others.

Gemstone, never underestimate the power of having or creating your *own space* to meditate, pray, and plan.

SEPTEMBER 12 GEM
Let the man pursue you.

Gemstone, you should not be on the prowl.

The man should be pursuing you, not the other way around—men love to chase but tend to run away if you're the one doing the chasing.

Instead, position yourself to be pursued by being in the places where you want a man with similar interests to find you.

Position yourself smartly:

- ✓ Let the man of intelligence find you in the public library.
- ✓ Let the man of exploration find you while traveling the world.
- ✓ Let the man of business find you in corporate settings.
- ✓ Let the man of niche groups (medical professionals, fitness trainers, biochemists, etc.) find you virtually on a safe and trusted dating app.
- ✓ Let the godly man find you in a place of worship.
- ✓ Let the wealthy man find you at an elite event.
- ✓ Let the man of exquisite taste find you while fine dining.

- ✓ Let the man of casualness find you while lounging.
- ✓ Let the man of construction and good with his hands find you in the hardware store or while out viewing & acquiring property.

SEPTEMBER 13 GEM
Never go wrong.

Gemstone, you'll *never go wrong* if you do what's right. Repeat the above statement until it sinks in.

SEPTEMBER 14 GEM
Immediately and suddenly.

Gemstone, *"immediately"* and *"suddenly"* are modern society's favorite two words.

While the things we want that come *immediately and suddenly* do indeed feel like the best things, don't discount what you can achieve with hard work—not only will taking the time to do that hard work lead to personal development, it will also drive results, spark the attention of others, bring you new opportunities, and sharpen your skills.

SEPTEMBER 15 GEM
10 fascinating facts about women.

1. Women speak 13,000 more words than men do daily.
2. Women can better rationalize than men can because of women's denser cerebral cortex.
3. Women survive traumatic injuries far more than men do due to women's hormones being able to enhance their immune systems.
4. Women's brains are designed to remember details better than men can.
5. Women experience "menstrual synchrony"—their monthly cycles sync up with their female relatives' and friends' cycles due to their pheromones.
6. On average, women live years longer than men do globally.
7. Women are sneakier and two to five times craftier than men, outwitting them more than often.
8. Women can see 20% more colors than men can.
9. Women can keep secrets way longer than men can.
10. Women spend nearly one year of their lives deciding what to wear.

Gemstone, the facts have it—you're quite *fascinating!*

SEPTEMBER 16 GEM
On a scale from 1 to 10.

Rate the overall way you feel about yourself *on a scale from 1 to 10.*

In order to give yourself an honest score, consider your intelligence, beauty, body image, health, talents, character, and how others perceive you.

Gemstone, whatever your score is, that is the maximum number you have invested into yourself. If you rate yourself a 7, then a 7 is exactly what you have personally invested into your overall self-image.

Think about your results and if you're satisfied with them.

If you're not satisfied with your results, determine where you can invest more into yourself to increase your self-evaluated personal rating.

SEPTEMBER 17 GEM
Light.

Sometimes things seem to "go to hell," as people like to say, before they improve. When things seem like they can't get any worse, they do.

Gemstone, the good thing is that there is *light* at the end of the tunnel.

Keep pressing towards that *light.*

SEPTEMBER 18 GEM
Utilitarianism.

Are you familiar with the term *"utilitarianism"*?

Utilitarianism means that an action taken is right if it benefits the most people involved. Many leaders become well-disciplined in this principle in order to make ethical decisions.

Use the following questions inspired by Joseph Badaracco's "Defining Moments: A Framework for Moral Decisions" Harvard lecture to measure the impact of your potential decision: Will you be Twitter's #1 trending topic for all the wrong reasons and turned into an internet meme, permanently? If roles were reversed and you were part of those impacted, would you think that the decision-maker was fair? Would you leave an "I agree with the decision that was made because it was fair" comment in their reviews section? Would the people you love and care about still stick around and support you after your decision, or would they be ashamed to be seen around you?

Gemstone, always seek to do the most right thing that will cause the least harm to the masses when making tough decisions.

SEPTEMBER 19 GEM
Do what you want.

You have the right to *do what you want* to do and live life how you want to live it.

Just remember that in *doing what you want*, there are always consequences, good or bad.

Make sure you're doing the right thing, Gemstone.

SEPTEMBER 20 GEM
Try it first.

Gemstone, if something does not go against your beliefs or values, *try it first* before dismissing it.

Taste new foods and delicacies, date interracially, try rappelling and parasailing, read quirky novels, visit your ancestral homeland, watch Bollywood and Sundance movies, dye your hair a different color, explore other careers, take a road trip across the country with your BFF, perform in front of large crowds, visit every continent, ride in a hot air balloon, cook an international meal, vacation solo, go camping to test out your survival skills, and more.

YOLO!

SEPTEMBER 21 GEM
Sleep well.

Strive to get a good night's sleep every night.

Your body restores itself when you're resting. The deeper the sleep, the deeper the restoration.

Sleep studies reveal that concentration improves, the body repairs itself, memories are stored, and so many other amazing things happen when you consistently get the sleep your body needs.

Most of all, Gemstone, the wise say that "God is doing work on your soul when you are in a deep sleep."

Don't miss out!

SEPTEMBER 22 GEM
8 random life hacks.

1. Make your bed! Your room will instantly look 60% cleaner.
2. For the best deals, book flights on early Tuesday mornings—airlines launch their discounts late on Monday nights.
3. Take melatonin if you're fighting being able to fall sleep. Off to dreamland you'll go!
4. Take a 100% caffeine pill (no sugar or artificial flavors) in the morning like athletes do to boost your morning workouts and overall performance without having the feeling of "crashing."
5. Turn important things you need to memorize into short tunes. Human memory works better with music and song.
6. Take pictures of your home when it's clean, then put them on poster boards or in a photo collage on your phone to show your spouse, kids, or room-mates exactly how each room in the home should look when they complete their chores. Then you'll get better cleaning results out of them.
7. Use accented letters like ã, í, ó in your passwords to make it extremely hard for anyone to guess them.
8. Reduce gray hairs by increasing your intake of vitamin B12.

Happy hacking, Gemstone!

SEPTEMBER 23 GEM
"Be all you can be."

You don't have to join the U.S. Army to *"Be all you can be."*

Though that route is a very plausible one, you can *be all you can be* when you begin to evolve as a person.

Own who you are and make becoming the best version of yourself a top priority.

Pursue personal development as much as possible, Gemstone! Seek opportunities that stretch you. Even more importantly, read more to expand your mind.

SEPTEMBER 24 GEM

There is no "I" in team.

That's a cliché yet very true statement.

Gemstone, take "I" out of the equation and surround yourself with a solid team or build one.

Stop trying to be a lone success in the workplace. That tends to never go too well, because as Steve Jobs said, "Great things in business are never done by one person. They're done by a team of people."

Successful people understand that it takes a strong network to be effective, impactful, and successful in the long term.

Maximize your team's strengths to get what needs to be done done. If you're riding a solo wave in the business place, be prepared to lose to the machine, a.k.a. the team.

Team = Together everyone achieves more!

SEPTEMBER 25 GEM
The ultimate litmus test.

So...you've been dating someone for a while and they're ready to take the relationship to the next level.

Gemstone, test their substance and morality first.

Perform the *ultimate litmus test:* ask yourself if the worst thing that could ever happen to you happened, would this person be the right person to hold your hand every step of the way? Would this person be the one to help you get through it?

If you cannot answer those questions with a hard "Yes!!" then you need to reconsider what you're about to dive into.

The answer is either "yes" or "no."

When performing this test to assess and measure the worthiness of a long-term relationship, there shouldn't be any in-between thoughts or irrational excuses.

SEPTEMBER 26 GEM
Date yourself.

Whether you're single or married, *date yourself.*

Treat yourself to date nights at the movies, five-course meals, comedy club shows, golfing, museums, picnics, sporting events, wineries, and lounging.

Gemstone, *dating yourself* means you're loving yourself.

You will learn so much more about yourself when you *date yourself!* And you will love yourself more and more, because no other human being can treat yourself better than you know how to treat yourself.

How so?

Because you know yourself best.

SEPTEMBER 27 GEM
Leave it in the drafts.

If you have even the remote inclination to not post something on your social media page, then you probably shouldn't.

It's better to leave a salacious, scandalous, or defamatory tweet, Facebook post, YouTube video, or Instagram post in the drafts if you have uncertainty about the impact and potential blowback of what you're posting.

Sit on it for a while. Even seek out the opinion of a trusted friend, because once that message is out there, it's out there. Backpedaling on a social media post? Well, that's kind of hard to do. To put it mildly.

Gemstone, unless you're a celebrity with amazing connections, unless you have plenty of money or insurance to pay victims for slander, unless you happen to know a dark webber who can scrape things off the 'net, unless you have a powerhouse publicist or know an "Olivia Pope" who can quickly clear things up...well, then maybe you're in the safe zone to post it, after all.

Then again, maybe not.

Post at your own risk, but be prepared for the potential consequences.

SEPTEMBER 28 GEM
Get in the door.

Sometimes you just need to *get in the door* first.

It's no secret you want to be in the C-suite. That will come in due time.

Get your foot in the door first, Gemstone, and then make it to the C-suite by consistently adding value to the company.

SEPTEMBER 29 GEM
False accusations.

If you're accused of being a liar, the genius way to put your accuser in check is by letting them know, "I didn't lie—I just didn't share."

Gemstone, everyone is not privy to your business and does not have the right to *falsely accuse* you of something just because they were not aware of your situation or because they didn't have all the details.

Whatever the situation, if it does not affect them, tell them to stop giving you grief and to respect your boundaries regarding how you share information and how you go about your personal business.

SEPTEMBER 30 GEM
The more, the better.

Doing more procedures makes better surgeons. Solving more mysteries makes better detectives. Tackling challenging projects makes better project managers. Taking more pictures makes better photographers. Reading more makes better readers. Pursuing intense training makes better athletes. Navigating rougher seas makes better sailors. Being more dedicated educators makes better teachers. Facing tougher opponents makes better players. Handling more cases makes better lawyers. Gathering greater details makes better storytellers. Flying long-distance flights makes better pilots. Doing endless research makes better scientists.

The same goes for you and the work you do: the more you do something and *the more* you do it with greater intent, *the better* at it you'll become.

Keep at it, Gemstone!

OCTOBER 1 GEM
24 hours.

Time is a commodity more valuable than money. Time has value because you spend it, and anything you spend has an associated cost. Every hour spent has a price tag hanging from it.

Dr. Myles Munroe states that "Time is a currency and is used to buy life. It is more important than money. If you're broke, you used your time to become broke. Time is so powerful that whatever you invest your time in, you become."

No matter their status or background, Gemstone, like you, everyone has the same *24 hours* in a day to make good use of their time. This is not up for argument—at its core it's a fact, measured from morning to nighttime—but what makes it different for everyone is how they spend their *24 hours.*

Ultimately, you waste time focusing on things that may be important but are not your passion.

The top three ways to make the most of your time are by engaging yourself in doing only what you desire; preserving your ideas, strategies, and priorities by sticking to them; and not trying to please and cater to everyone.

OCTOBER 2 GEM
Clean out the yuck.

Whatever you need to do, get a mental cleansing.

Get a mental colonic, mental enema, mental senna, mental suppository, mental prebiotic, mental probiotic, mental fiber supplement, or mental osmotic.

All of these things sound mentally invasive, but they symbolically describe what it will take to clear all the negativity out of your mind.

Gemstone, seek therapy to gain mental clarity, try yoga for mental calmness, and practice mindfulness to hardwire your brain for untroubledness.

Clean out the yuck!

OCTOBER 3 GEM
Do it with a smile.

There are a lot of things in life we have to do but really just don't feel like doing. Yet there's no real way of getting around it—if we don't do it, we'll suffer the consequences of inaction.

Going to work, cooking, cleaning, studying for a class, paying bills, tending to children, working on a project, getting an oil change, etc. are just some of the mundane things that have to get done.

Surprisingly, there's a way to make doing those things seem less draining, and that's by *doing them with a smile*.

Commit to smiling through some of the things you really are tired of, don't feel like doing, or even hate doing.

When you *do it with a smile*, that instantly begins to make you feel better about doing it as you get into it. Your body positively reacts to your smile since your brain associates smiling with pleasurable things.

So smile away, Gemstone!

OCTOBER 4 GEM

No one else is more qualified.

It's a scientific fact that your DNA can never be duplicated.

You are 100% you, and there can never be another you. You were made with no mistakes.

Researchers from Stockholm University and the Manchester University NHS Foundation Trust discovered that the "egg effectively chooses the sperm it wants" out of the millions of other swimmers.

There you have it! The egg purposely chose you. "Put me in, Coach!" yelled the sperm that helped create you as it approached the egg.

This confirms that *no one else is more qualified* to be you but you.

So, Gemstone, be you.

OCTOBER 5 GEM
Crabs in a barrel.

Is everyone in your circle passive-aggressively fighting each other so that no one wins?

There's enough room for everyone to be successful, but fighting each other at ground zero will keep everyone at ground zero.

This *crabs in a barrel* mentality hurts all those in the bucket—none of the crabs can climb up because all the crabs are continuously clawing each other right back down.

Don't be crabby, Gemstone.

OCTOBER 6 GEM
Your love language.

According to Gary Chapman, author of *The 5 Love Languages,* everyone has a love language.

Simply put, people define and show love differently from one another.

Is *your love language* French while his is Spanish? You'll know that your love for each other is suffering from the "Tower of Babel" effect (Gen 11:9) if you find yourselves constantly questioning each other's love.

Contrary to what you may believe or feel equates to showing love, your significant other may not view it as love when you tell them "You are so great!" Instead, your significant other may define and receive love by having your undivided attention or by receiving your physical love and affection.

On the other hand, you may consider love to be gestures in the form of receiving flowers, cards, candy, and occasional lavish gifts or trips...or in the form of just them watching the kids while you enjoy some "me time."

Gemstone, communicate *your love language* to your partner! And learn theirs, too, so that you both can meet each other's needs of what it means to be loved.

OCTOBER 7 GEM
No shortcuts.

Gemstone, do the work!

Stop trying to take shortcuts, because taking short-cuts results in inefficiencies, poor quality, and do-overs.

Push through the process! It's very rewarding on the other side.

OCTOBER 8 GEM
"I do."

You desperately want to say *"I do"* and marry the man of your dreams, but you've already said *"I do"* to many other things in life that you'll need to clear up first.

Gemstone, you're in a few marriages already.

"What marriages?" you ask.

You're in a work marriage, a single life marriage, a social media marriage, a personal goals marriage, a travel marriage, a sports and fitness marriage, an entre-preneurship marriage, a business goals marriage, a "me, myself, and I" marriage, and more.

What separations or divorces are you willing to make to commit to the real thing?

Marriage is real work. When you say *"I do"* to your spouse, they become your priority. Other things still have importance, but your spouse and the family you have or plan to create with them must come first.

OCTOBER 9 GEM
Dream big!

Your dreams should be big, so big that it will take incredible faith for them to come true.

It's satisfying to know that your biggest and wildest dreams have little to no competition because your vision is so intricately detailed, designed, and assigned to you.

Write your vision out in full detail on paper because if it's not written down, it's only imagination—making your vision invalid.

Gemstone, know that you are fully capable of achieving your biggest dreams by putting your faith to work.

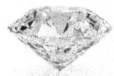

OCTOBER 10 GEM
Sit your crazy-tail self down!

Why do you feel the need to speak to people in that manner?

Why do you feel it's okay to scream and yell to get your point across? Why are you making a scene every time you don't get your way? Why are you gaslighting people? Why are you so passive-aggressive in your relationships? Why do you feel the need to habitually lie? Why do you refuse to take accountability for your actions? Why are you cursing out people who work in the store? Why are you constantly trolling and bullying others on social media? Why are you throwing rocks and hiding your hands? Why are you getting your nails done but driving around on empty? Why are you manipulating people? Why are you not scheduling your annual physicals and exams? Why are you messing around with someone you know is already spoken for? Why do you pride yourself on being messy? Why do you refuse to eat healthier and exercise? Why do you think you should never have to work for anything? Why do you always want to argue or physically fight someone just because they made you mad?

...Why, why, and why? Just why?

Gemstone, is any of that you? If so, you're exhibiting out-of-control behavior.

Sit your crazy-tail self all the way down!

OCTOBER 11 GEM
The greatest distance.

Misunderstanding is *the greatest distance* between two people.

If differences are not met with grace, patience, and compassion, those differences separate individuals and put them further and further away from one another.

Gemstone, commit to avoid misunderstanding those you hold close to your heart! As the writer Elias Canetti said, "Understanding, as we understand it, is misunderstanding."

Let your communication keep you close.

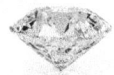

OCTOBER 12 GEM
Take a break.

Taking a break from the people you love and care about when they work your nerves is necessary.

Communicate to them that you need time for peace and to process. The short break you take from others when they irritate you is the reset you may need.

During this time, take advantage of pondering unin-terrupted and undistorted viewpoints through medita-tion. Go for a long walk, ride a bike, practice yoga, read a good book, and take naps to help unnerve yourself.

Gemstone, after your time of peace and processing—and when things are calm again and tensions have sub-sided—then take the time to clear the air with those you love in order for you all to move forward.

Preserve your nerves by *taking a break*.

OCTOBER 13 GEM
Learn from them.

Gemstone, there is a lesson in almost everything.

It is not a coincidence that you sat on the outskirts of a situation as it unraveled before your eyes. Though that situation may not have directly involved you, you were able to spectate and observe from the sidelines what went right, what went wrong, or both.

Take every life experience, problem, and issue you are aware of and *learn from them*. Gauge how to avoid or handle similar situations down the road.

OCTOBER 14 GEM
Have a personal strategic plan.

Gemstone, you need a well-devised plan to reach your goals.

Take note of the strategic business plan model. Its desired key outcomes connect to the organization's mission, vision, and values, and the plan drives sustainability through generating constant innovations and competitive advantages.

The CEO monitors the internal and external forces that impact the organization's performance and makes changes to the strategy when needed.

Like an organization, you should *have a personal strategic plan*. The plan needs to be a well-crafted road map that outlines the steps you'll take to achieve your goals. These steps should be aligned with your personal mission, vision, and values and also allow you to be agile for greater self-resiliency.

Your personal strategic plan will help you focus your energies on achieving what's most important to you.

OCTOBER 15 GEM
Map it out.

Whatever you wish to accomplish in life, envision it in your mind.

Gemstone, play those accomplishments through completely from beginning to end in your mind! *Map out* exactly how you plan to achieve your life goals.

When you begin to mentally play out what you desire, you begin to attract those things. Why? Because the human mind shapes what you are visualizing into reality.

OCTOBER 16 GEM
Set your reminders.

Gemstone, you have so many things going on in your life that you're not going to remember everything all the time (unless maybe you've been taking ginkgo biloba daily faithfully for years).

Set your reminders in your phone or on your Alexa or Google device, your Outlook and Google calendars, or even your daily planner.

Don't forget about the important things you need to get done just because you forgot to write them down!

If you write it down, it happens; if you don't, it won't.

OCTOBER 17 GEM
Yes Day

Gemstone, pick a day at least once or twice a year for yourself as being your *Yes Day!*

On that day, say "Yes" to yourself about everything.

Empower yourself by saying "Yes!" all day long:

- ✓ Yes to pizza and dessert for breakfast.
- ✓ Yes to calling out of work to relax for the day.
- ✓ Yes to the new hair color.
- ✓ Yes to the new outfit.
- ✓ Yes to the overnight babysitter.
- ✓ Yes to the blind date.
- ✓ Yes to getting in the bed at 4 p.m. loaded up with snacks.
- ✓ Yes to the exquisite meal.
- ✓ Yes to joy riding.
- ✓ Yes to an all day spa day.
- ✓ Yes to doing no chores.
- ✓ Yes to catching up on all your favorite shows & movies.
- ✓ Yes to exploring that new town.
- ✓ Yes to that shopping spree.
- ✓ Yes to saying "No" to everyone else's requests for the day but your own.

It's your *Yes Day*, so say "Yes, yes, yes, yes, and yes!"

OCTOBER 18 GEM

The world has enough critics.

Gemstone, aren't you tired of those who always have something negative to say?

Those people bleed hate—if you sliced them open, hate would ooze out. And if you're a self-criticizer, you're one of them.

Psychologists say that human beings can be their own worst critics. You have enough known and unknown critics already, so don't be another one of them.

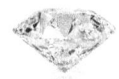

OCTOBER 19 GEM
Easy money grabs.

Gemstone, extra money-making opportunities are endless.

Today's 16 easy money grabs:

1. Rideshare services: Uber, Lyft
2. Grocery shoppers/deliverers: Instacart, Amazon Fresh
3. Online surveys: SurveyJunkie.com
4. Online notary: Notarize.com, Notarylive.com
5. Virtual focus groups: FocusGroups.org, FocusGroups.com
6. Renting out your property, room, or space Airbnb, Verbo
7. House sitting: Housesitter.com, Care.com
8. Plasma donating: BioLife.com, CSLPlasma.com
9. Specialized skills: Thumbtack.com, Freelancer.com
10. Event gigs: GigSalad.com
11. Virtual assistance: Upwork.com
12. Teaching online: VIPKid.com, Outschool.com
13. Facebook Ad Manager for small businesses: Facebook.com
14. TikTok's Creator Fund: Tiktok.com
15. YouTube content creator: YouTube.com
16. Instagram influencer: Instagram.com

Good luck racking up those extra coins!

OCTOBER 20 GEM
A proper burial.

Who upset you? Who caused you hurt, pain, and turmoil? Who angered you or manipulated you and never apologized?

Whoever that person is, write out on paper exactly what they did to you. Be descriptive in writing out how displeased and disgusted you are with them and put them in their place in your letter. Leave no stone unturned in expressing exactly how you feel.

Get all those bottled-up feelings on paper, because when it's on paper, you are releasing those feelings.

Then give those feelings written on paper *a proper burial* by throwing your written paper into the fireplace or bonfire, ripping it up, putting it in the trashcan, flushing it down the toilet, or putting it into a crosscut paper shredder.

Give your hurt and pain that someone else caused *a proper burial* Gemstone—to get the closure you need.

OCTOBER 21 GEM
Time to leave.

When you're in an environment where you are constantly disrespected, taken for granted, and ridiculed—an environment where your ideas are laughed at and are unappreciated—it's *time to leave.*

People become products of toxic environments if they stick around in them for too long. So, vacate environments that are not conducive to your mental health and overall well-being.

Gemstone, respect who you are and act on that inner nudge to leave when you must. Leaving is self-preservation.

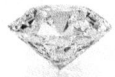

OCTOBER 22 GEM
Who do you look at first?

When you've taken a group picture and then you look at it, *who do you look at first?*

Yourself.

You inspect yourself first to see how you look and if it's a worthy picture to keep or share before you check out how everyone else looks.

This is because you care about your self-image.

When you begin to stop caring about your appearance—especially in pictures that will be shared by others with others—then you stop caring about your self-image.

Gemstone, never stop caring about how you "show up."

OCTOBER 23 GEM
Watch your mouth.

Your words are not meaningless. On the contrary, they are very heavy and very powerful. Your words have energy, and energy never dies; it's only recreated.

God himself created the world with His words (Psa. 33:6).

Do not use your words to tear down, destroy, or spread lies or hate. Instead, Gemstone, use your words to love, help, heal, and forgive.

OCTOBER 24 GEM
What's not *replaceable.*

Material things are replaceable, but the people you genuinely love and care about are not.

Gemstone, treat the ones you love with loving kindness and gratefulness, because what makes them who they are to you can never be 100% duplicated by anyone else.

Ever.

OCTOBER 25 GEM
Happy pill.

Don't forget to take your *happy pill* today, Gemstone!
Your dosage of mental happiness should be taken every day.

Happy pill supplemental facts:

- ✓ Big smile.
- ✓ Cheerfulness.
- ✓ Gracefulness.
- ✓ Patience.
- ✓ Kindness.
- ✓ Trustworthiness.
- ✓ Positiveness.
- ✓ Humor.
- ✓ Friendliness.
- ✓ Gratefulness.
- ✓ Sociability.
- ✓ Self-confidence.
- ✓ Gentleness.
- ✓ High energy.
- ✓ Purposefulness.

WARNING: A double dosage may be needed for severe bad attitudes.

OCTOBER 26 GEM
"Pushin' P."

This relatively new saying taken from the urban vernacular is really about the positive things you're focused on and pushing to make happen in life.

What positive things are you pushin'?

Are you pushin' purpose, prosperity, peace, patience, philanthropy, popularity, prettiness, power, passion, perseverance, plenty, plushness, poise, poshness, and prestige?

Gemstone, *keep pushin' those Ps!*

OCTOBER 27 GEM
Your worst enemy.

Gemstone, would you be surprised to know that *your worst enemy* is closer than you think?

Matter of fact, *your worst enemy* is attached to your body. It is near the lower part of your face where food is consumed and where speech and sounds are emitted. Yes, it's your mouth.

Your worst enemy is your mouth.

Stop saying bad things about yourself and tearing yourself down. Instead, make your mouth become your cheerleader.

Let your mouth speak positively about your life, who you are, your greatnesses, and your successes.

OCTOBER 28 GEM
20/10 vision.

20/20 vision is the standard—it's rare for people to have *20/10 vision.* That's the ability to see clearly from a distance of 20 feet.

Having *20/10 vision* is phenomenal, because things farther away are clearer to you than they are to the average person with their average vision. This innate trait allows 3% of the world's population to sharply see the bigger picture.

Gemstone, how can you gain such *20/10* clarity in your overall life?

5 strategies to implement 20/10 vision in your life:

1. Declutter your living and work environment often and create space to process.
2. Silence the mental chatter through daily 5 to 10 minute meditations to rid yourself of internal and external distractions.
3. Be in the moment—immerse yourself in whatever you're doing. If you're reading a book, read a book with no TV or phone playing in the background. If you're eating, focus only on the food you're eating: the color of it, the aroma of it, the taste of it.

4. Remove distractions by silencing notifications: turn off the TV, music, and any other device that interferes with your focus.
5. Be where you need to be. If you want to paint, for example, be in front of a canvas with a paintbrush in your hand.

OCTOBER 29 GEM

Get right back up on the horse.

Okay, so you missed a day. No worries! Life happens and can throw you off schedule.

It's okay, Gemstone—it happens to even the best of us. *Get right back up on the horse* the next day and ride out and stick to your plan.

Being thrown off for a day or two is not the end-all and be-all as long as you don't allow a gap of time to completely thwart you and cause you to start back at square one.

Saddle up and shout "Yee-haw!"

OCTOBER 30 GEM
Code-switching.

Code-switching is the art of being able to sit in authenticity and be part of every room you walk into.

A woman's ability to *code-switch* shows off her complexities and humanistic range of abilities that allow her to connect with diverse groups of people. One minute you may be wearing your corporate hat; the next your philanthropic cap; the next your socialite shoes.

Code-switching is an art. It's a skill acquired through gaining varying levels of education, pursuing continuous learning and growing opportunities, building relationships, and exploring cultural connections.

Gemstone, become adept at *code-switching!* Then you'll be able to adapt to and navigate through any personal or business setting to advance your network and net worth.

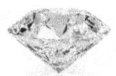

OCTOBER 31 GEM
Come out from behind their shadows.

Gemstone, it's safe to come out now—*stop hiding behind someone else's shadow.*

You've been in obscurity long enough and are just as good as they are...if not better.

Own your greatness, share your talents, voice your opinions, and drive the energy and attention to yourself.

It's time!

Only those whom you're standing behind who don't want to see you elevated will despise you when you come out from behind their shadows.

NOVEMBER 1 GEM
Chess moves.

Making *chess moves* in life is creating a strategy for long-term winning.

The key is to play the board for your own advantages and not solely just as defenses against the actions of other players. In other words, be proactive in life versus reactive.

Your moves should always be intentional (refer to the August 28th Gem). Come to the chessboard with a strategy and then follow through on it.

Gemstone, your end goal is not only to win in life but to possess sustainability—which is brilliance.

Checkmate.

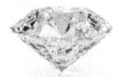

NOVEMBER 2 GEM

"Men-" problems.

- ✓ Menstrual cramps.
- ✓ Menopause.
- ✓ Mental illness.
- ✓ Meningitis.
- ✓ Meniscus tear.
- ✓ Meningococcal disease.
- ✓ Meniere's disease.
- ✓ Menetrier disease.
- ✓ Mendelson syndrome.
- ✓ Menkes syndrome.
- ✓ Menorrhagia.

Gemstone, how ironic that so many women's problems, diseases, and injuries start with "men-"!

Oh, sigh!

NOVEMBER 3 GEM
P.U.S.H.

"If you don't believe in something,
you will fall for anything."
—Alexander Hamilton

Many successful people today pray daily because they are firm believers that prayer changes things.

Find a great person, and they will show you their faith. They are unashamed to share how they *P.U.S.H.* through.

They do not doubt there is a higher being and they do not doubt that their prayers and the prayers of others have helped carry them through.

Gemstone, as the great evangelist DLM says, "Pray until something happens."

P.U.S.H.!

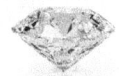

NOVEMBER 4 GEM
"That didn't age well."

Watch your mouth, because the words that come out of it are given life once spoken.

If you're about to say something that you know you'll regret saying when you look back to reflect on it, then don't say it.

There are enough examples out there already to learn from, Gemstone.

Google *"That didn't age well"* and see for yourself.

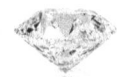

NOVEMBER 5 GEM

The percentage of your correction.

Gemstone, the percentage of whatever you're able to correct in life is the percentage of your personal effectiveness.

If you did a 360° on being a messy person—which landed you right back at being a messy person—then your overall effectiveness of being a decent person is just 50%.

But if you made a 180° and did a complete turnaround (refer to the January 7th Gem) and are no longer a "messy" person, then your overall effectiveness of being a decent person is 100%.

100% of your correction = 100% of your effectiveness.

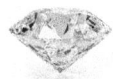

NOVEMBER 6 GEM
Meet people where they are.

Gemstone, if you care about people, then connect with them on the level they're at.

If they're uneducated, communicate with them on a level they'll comprehend. If they're not into politics, then speak generally to them when political topics come up. If they lack business sense, speak to them in layman's terms to get your point across.

Meet people where they are.

Get to know them! In time, they will begin to learn from you and appreciate the value-add you are to their life.

NOVEMBER 7 GEM
Traffic jams.

Being stuck in a *traffic jam* is usually the worst and always happens at the most inopportune time, as in when you really need to get somewhere.

Not going anywhere for a while, Gemstone? Well, neither are the other drivers stuck on the freeway with you.

Don't waste time yelling at other drivers, excessively honking your horn, cutting anybody off, flicking anybody off, or playing "Move B—Get Out Da Way" by Ludacris.

Leave this behavior to those filled with road rage or who are just immature.

Use your valuable *traffic jam* time to learn! Connect to your car's Bluetooth to access your audio content like audiobooks and informative podcasts on topics that can help you learn and grow.

Take advantage of this time stuck on the highway to get yourself one step closer to achieving your dreams.

NOVEMBER 8 GEM
Don't poke the bear.

Gemstone, if you decide to cross that line to purposely anger and upset someone, don't be surprised when they respond with "guns ablazin'."

Stop mistaking people's kindness, quietness, and positioning for weakness.

There comes a point where enough is enough, and when it's enough, it's enough and that's enough.

Poking the bear just might get you clawed.

NOVEMBER 9 GEM
No connection.

Once you've confirmed that *you don't have a connection* with someone, stop pushing the envelope. Don't force what's not there.

Cut your losses and move on, Gemstone! Save your time and energy for people who do connect with you.

People who vibe with you, vibe with you; those who don't, won't.

NOVEMBER 10 GEM
Keep believing.

Life's obstacles can leave a sour taste in your mouth, one that hinders your faith and thought processes. But this is not the time to regress!

It's time to *keep believing* and forging ahead.

To *keep believing*, Gemstone, you must push past self-doubt, push past your insecurities, and never give up. The moment you stop believing, the possibilities of what you desire will cease.

You're closer than you think you are.

So, *keep believing* and don't allow life's obstacles to persuade you to give up on your dreams.

NOVEMBER 11 GEM
Mine, mine, mine.

Keep a few things to yourself that are just for you.

Humble and generous people tend to struggle to not feel guilty for things they don't want to share.

But you are entitled to have those special things all to yourself, Gemstone! If someone wants it, don't give it to them.

Instead, tell them where they can go get it.

NOVEMBER 12 GEM
Top five.

Gemstone, in every interview, sell yourself by sharing the *top five* reasons why you are the best person for the job and the *top five* reasons why you should secure the position.

Your top five reasons should include the following:

1. Explain how your skills and experience connect to the organization's overall strategy.
2. Tell them how you will quickly connect to the organization's people and work culture. Share your previous track record of successfully having done so before.
3. Share actual metrics and results you've produced for prior companies and how you plan to drive results for this company if given the opportunity.
4. Explain the professional development milestones, certifications, and continuous educational initiatives you've achieved that specifically link to the opportunity in front of you right now.
5. Provide a solid example of how you have led, managed, or coached a team through the art of short storytelling. This will communicate your ability to lead and develop others.

NOVEMBER 13 GEM
Can you do it?

Gemstone, when you hear *"Can you do it?"* that's not really the question that's being asked.

The question is really this: can you place the letter "I" at the beginning of the question and remove the word "you" from the middle of it—and change the question mark to an exclamation point—to make the question into a very bold and convincing statement?

"I can do it!"—And remember, whether you say you "can" do it or whether you say you "can't" do it, you're always right.

NOVEMBER 14 GEM
Until...

Gemstone, when you say, "I do" to your spouse, the commitment should hopefully be forever and not *"until..."*

"Until..." is the reason why 50% of marriages end in divorce.

Until reasons:

- ✓ Until he gets on your nerves. (Which he will.)
- ✓ Until he misuses finances by making a huge purchase without consulting with you. (Potentially he will.)
- ✓ Until he forgets to do something. (Which he will.)
- ✓ Until he stares too long at a beautiful woman walking by in the grocery store. (Not too far-fetched.)
- ✓ Until he forgets to pick up the kids from childcare. (Potentially he will.)
- ✓ Until he hangs out in his man cave for too long. (Which he will.)
- ✓ Until he's emotionally unavailable to you. (Potentially he will.)
- ✓ Until he forgets your birthday or anniversary. (Potentially he will.)

Make sure you understand the ebbs and flows of a relationship before you decide to make a forever commitment and say "I do."

NOVEMBER 15 GEM
Gaslighting.

If something happened and it affected you or made you feel "some kind of way" and the other person is vocally dismissive of the fact that your emotional state was impacted, then that person is 100% *gaslighting* you.

Call them out on it every time, because *gaslighting is gaslighting,* and it's very problematic behavior.

Gemstone, your feelings and emotions are real! Those close to you should not disregard them and act as if they're not real.

NOVEMBER 16 GEM
Increase your baseline.

Increase your personal baseline year over year to improve your personal performance.

If your first year's goal is to read 10 books, then your following year's baseline should increase and you should aim to read 12 to 13 books.

If your Year One goal is to walk daily for 30 minutes, then your Year Two goal should be to walk daily for 45 minutes.

If your goal is to participate in a three-month program or certification process, then afterward, set yourself on accomplishing an even more challenging program or a more prestigious certification that will take longer to complete.

Gemstone, focus on *increasing your personal baseline* by small increments year over year in order to achieve sustainable personal growth.

NOVEMBER 17 GEM
Ghosting.

If the person you're dating abruptly stops reaching out to you and you know that they're okay and weren't hit by a bus or lost at sea, then they are *ghosting* you.

Their complete silence and unresponsive behavior without giving you any notice that they were going to fall off the map is a clear sign that you've dodged a bullet.

Ghosting is very childish and deplorable behavior. It's a disgusting trait and a foul way of treating people.

Gemstone, you have standards and you love yourself, so refrain from going on a ghost hunt! Don't waste your time searching for a "ghoster."

Avoid emotional roller coasters by leaving those bad spooky spirits alone—chasing ghosts never ends well.

Ghost him back by moving on.

NOVEMBER 18 GEM
Rearview mirror.

Everything is smaller in your *rearview mirror.* Why? Because you've passed what's behind you.

Think about it—95% of the time, your car's gear is in "drive" and not in "reverse." Gemstone, remember, you are driving forward and not backward.

Leave what's behind you behind you. Focus only on what's ahead of you—what's on the other side of your huge front windshield.

Cross the bridge, veer to the right, pay the toll, and keep going. Buckle up and accelerate for a fun and adventurous life ahead!

NOVEMBER 19 GEM
Change looks like...

- ✓ Change looks like finally going on that blind date.
- ✓ Change looks like choosing a baked or grilled dinner versus a fried dinner.
- ✓ Change looks like waking up one hour earlier to work out.
- ✓ Change looks like finally deleting that one number off your phone.
- ✓ Change looks like putting your name in the hat.
- ✓ Change looks like going on that dream trip.
- ✓ Change looks like purging your home of old stuff.
- ✓ Change looks like replacing trash TV with informative books and videos.
- ✓ Change looks like finally starting that business.
- ✓ Change looks better than yesterday.

Change looks good on you, Gemstone!

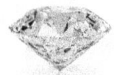

NOVEMBER 20 GEM
Mediocrity has no place.

Stop settling for minimal and unimpressive standards! Instead, set the bar high.

Gemstone, have dignity, self-respect, and pride in your output and your ability to produce stellar work. Care enough about the quality of your work and how you show up, because *mediocrity should have no place* in your life.

NOVEMBER 21 GEM
"Talk that talk!"

The saying *"Talk that talk!"* means to speak fluently, confidently, and boastfully about yourself or about something you know to be real or true in order to make a point.

Gemstone, it's time to flex on 'em! Brag a little. Just a little—*solo un poco.*

Let them know who you are, because there's nothing wrong with doing so. In her lyrics, Barbadian singer Rhianna says, "Everything I do is big / I talk big money, I talk big homes / I sell out arenas..." Clearly, RiRi was in her "bag" during this song. She's called "Badazz RiRi" for a reason.

The one thing Rihanna is going to do is *"Talk that talk,"* because she's strikingly self-assured in who she is, what she can do, and what she brings to the table. You should be self-assured, too!

"Talk that talk" today and remind those who need a friendly reminder exactly who you are in case they forgot.

NOVEMBER 22 GEM
You're stuck with you.

Gemstone, the one thing *you're stuck with is you.*

There's no way of getting around it.

You can make all the physical changes to your body you want, but none of those will change that you are you.

You are who you are and *you are stuck with you,* so love yourself and be your own best version of yourself.

NOVEMBER 23 GEM
Live with expectations.

- ✓ Wake up trusting the sun to shine.
- ✓ Keep your phone nearby anticipating that it will ring.
- ✓ Open your mailbox believing that the offer letter is there.
- ✓ Check your email knowing that you'll receive the confirmation.
- ✓ Turn on the TV looking forward to hearing good news.
- ✓ Open your front door expecting a delivery.
- ✓ Answer the call counting on the news to be in your favor.
- ✓ Scroll down your computer screen believing that you'll find what you're looking for.
- ✓ Open the envelope believing that letter says yes.
- ✓ Dream like it's coming true.
- ✓ Turn the page expecting to find your answer.
- ✓ Hold the keys trusting its yours.
- ✓ Pray like you know it's going to happen.
- ✓ Say "Thank you" as if it already happened.

Gemstone, live expecting that all the wonderful things you believe in and imagine will happen, because when you *live with expectations*, you are preparing yourself to receive those wonderful things.

NOVEMBER 24 GEM
Write the end first.

Before pursuing your goals in life, imagine what your life would look like if you were to accomplish those goals. How? By *writing the end first.*

Gemstone, what do you anticipate your life will be like?

Writing the end first allows you to stay focused by keeping the end in mind throughout the journey.

Authors and screenwriters write the end of their stories first, movie directors often shoot the end of their movies first, architects design buildings before they're built, and God himself even declares the end from the beginning (Isa. 46:10).

Writing the end first serves as a constant reminder of what can be if you don't give up.

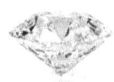

NOVEMBER 25 GEM
No legal U-turns.

You're leaving a bad situation for good because what you thought was the case is not so and who you thought they were they are not.

They've given you a preview of the future of what things will be like if you stick around, and it's not good. You're only guaranteed more of the same of what you're currently experiencing.

As Maya Angelou said, Gemstone, "When someone shows you who they are, believe them—the first time."

Hop onto the freeway, because you will find *no legal U-turns* to take you back into a bad situation.

There's no going back!

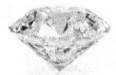

NOVEMBER 26 GEM
In and out.

As educationalist CBM says, "Garbage in, garbage out."

But this philosophy goes beyond the physical effects and outward appearance of what your mouth consumes and your body digests.

The saying also speaks to what you mentally consume and absorb.

What you continuously take in will begin to contribute to the characteristics of who you are as a person. If you excessively ingurgitate messes, then those same messes will begin to show up in your behavior.

Are you consuming trash TV 24/7, keeping company with toxic people, listening to self-destructive and coded music lyrics that are vile, constantly allowing others to manipulate you, lying, having excessively negative thoughts, acting jealously, and behaving selfishly? If so, then what you are mentally devouring is not good.

What's been consumed will begin to rear its ugly head, because what's in you eventually comes out—after all, it has latched onto the essence and makeup of who you are.

Gemstone, engage in things that are of substance and have an awareness of things that are not.

NOVEMBER 27 GEM

"Something in the milk ain't clean."

When situations look and smell sour to you, more than likely, your senses are not fooling you.

The story doesn't add up! As the saying goes, *"Something in the milk ain't clean."*

Gemstone, trust your senses and allow them to serve their purpose of gathering and responding to information about an environment or situation. This will aid your perception and survival.

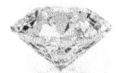

NOVEMBER 28 GEM
Your safe word.

What's *your safe word* for signaling a spouse, relative, or friend to come bail you out of undesirable and uncomfortable conversations and situations?

Establish *your safe word* so that you can comfortably "exit stage left," so to speak, thanks to the carefully crafted interruption of your trusted person.

Gemstone, don't stick around and entertain nonsense when you have an "out"!

"Coco Chanel," "Pineapple Express," "Charlie's Angels," "Pandora's Box," and "Zenith" are a few safe words people have used to get bailed out of unwanted situations.

Be crafty and come up with a safe word today.

NOVEMBER 29 GEM
Tap in.

Going from an unconscious to a conscious state of mind and coming into a higher frequency and vibration is called *"tapping in."*

Gemstone, rise above with a higher mindset.

Tap into your awareness and surroundings and fully activate your mental faculties.

Tap in to a "higher" understanding.

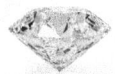

NOVEMBER 30 GEM
What others will say.

Some therapists have their patients write their own eulogy to have them better understand the essence of who they are by *what others will say* about them when it's all said and done.

Though many people might respect the goal of such an assignment, writing your eulogy may not align with your beliefs about living a long life. Or perhaps you might find writing your eulogy to be a very superstitious thing to do.

But Gemstone, no matter your age, shift your mindset and compose a reflection of who you are when you look at who you are today and who you desire to be in the future.

Write in the third person to truly hear how you anticipate your life's story to unfold and how others will share it in memory of you. That way, you're still accomplishing the goal of capturing and understanding the essence of yourself without an accompanying narrative that you're channeling your eternal rest.

DECEMBER 1 GEM
Recondition your thinking.

The negative words you've spoken about yourself over the years are like internal bleeding. This non-self-serving diabolical behavior is destroying you from the inside out.

To get out of this vicious cycle of self-destruction, you must *recondition your thinking* by conditioning your mind with positive words and affirmations (refer to the January 31 Gem). Also, even when you don't feel like it, you need to speak those positive words aloud.

For every negative word that continues to spew out of your mouth, immediately replace it with three positive words.

Remember, it takes about 21 days to change a bad habit. Let today be Day One, Gemstone.

DECEMBER 2 GEM
Allegedly.

- ✓ Allegedly, he cheated on his ex.
- ✓ Allegedly, he's a liar.
- ✓ Allegedly, he went to jail.
- ✓ Allegedly, he was fired from his job.
- ✓ Allegedly, he leases and doesn't own.
- ✓ Allegedly, he's a womanizer.
- ✓ Allegedly, he's on the down low.
- ✓ Allegedly, he's passive-aggressive.
- ✓ Allegedly, he's unfaithful.
- ✓ Allegedly, he's financially irresponsible.
- ✓ Allegedly, he's boring.
- ✓ Allegedly, he's a mama's boy.
- ✓ Allegedly, he's unstable to be in a relationship.
- ✓ Allegedly, he's already spoken for.
- ✓ Allegedly, he's emotionally unavailable.
- ✓ Allegedly, he's a deadbeat father.
- ✓ Allegedly, he barely can make ends-meet.
- ✓ Allegedly, he's back to his old ways.

Gemstone, go beyond the allegations and get the facts yourself instead of automatically believing hearsay. Then proceed with the relationship accordingly.

DECEMBER 3 GEM
Dysfunctional normalcy.

Maladjusted living is comfortably living with drama, problems, or stress or neglecting your beliefs and values by accepting someone in your life who refuses to take responsibility for their toxic behavior.

None of this is normal.

Gemstone, if this is the way you are functionally living, then your dysfunction has become your normalcy.

Stop being comfortable living in your dysfunction! That kind of tolerance and acceptance of negative behavior is cause for concern.

Seek professional help to find ways to escape *dysfunctional normalcy* so that you can live in peace and tranquility with others.

DECEMBER 4 GEM
Against your better judgment.

You know better! You've been there and done that, but yet you allow it anyway.

You accept calls from the habitual cheater. You continue to watch psychological horror movies that give you nightmares for months. You spend money on unnecessary, lavish items while knowing that you can barely pay your bills.

It's time to stop going *against your better judgment.*

You know what's best, because your past mistakes have taught you valuable lessons already. You just need to apply lessons learned to your life going forward!

Use your better judgment, Gemstone. You have it for a reason.

DECEMBER 5 GEM
Sorry, not sorry.

Gemstone, do you find yourself apologizing for everything?

Is saying "I'm sorry" your natural response to people versus being honest about how you truly feel? So much apologizing—especially for things you truly mean to say or do—is being "fake" and it's just downright overkill. In reality, you may not be sorry for something, but saying "I'm sorry" has become your clutch.

Sadly, habitual apologizers even apologize for their own existence, which is very self-deprecating.

Instead of apologizing, how about using the phrases "My bad," "Oops," "Oh, wow," "Poor thing," "That's unfortunate," "I said what I said," or "I'm being transparent."

Apologize when necessary but stop saying you're sorry when you're not. Not only does that make you look insecure to others, many find excessive apologizing to be unauthentic and aggravating.

DECEMBER 6 GEM
Plan it.

You know the saying "If you didn't post it on social media, it didn't happen"? Although this isn't quite as true, there's a similar saying: "If you don't *plan it*, it won't happen."

Plan your day by planning your tasks. You will have a greater chance of accomplishing more if you plan what you have to get done. Why? The human brain functions better when our responsibilities are structured. *Planning* will free you from the anxiety that comes from tasks you haven't completed that are distracting you, according to *The Guardian's* 2017 published article, "The Psychology of the To-Do list—Why Your Brain Loves Ordered Tasks."

Gemstone, not having a plan = having a plan to fail.

DECEMBER 7 GEM

Not man enough.

- ✓ Dishonest.
- ✓ Deceitful.
- ✓ Uncommitted.
- ✓ Disrespectful.
- ✓ Unambitious.
- ✓ Jobless.
- ✓ Transportation-less.
- ✓ Impatient.
- ✓ Faithless.
- ✓ Egotistical.
- ✓ Incredulous.
- ✓ Unethical.
- ✓ Disorderly.
- ✓ Offensive.
- ✓ Disloyal.
- ✓ Unstable.
- ✓ Hateful.
- ✓ Weak-minded.
- ✓ Narcissistic.

Gemstone, *he's not man enough* for you.
On to the next!

DECEMBER 8 GEM
Background checks.

Always perform a *background check* on the person you are seriously dating or plan to marry.

It will be well worth the $60 to $100 you'll spend. You will have peace of mind knowing your partner's financial history and if they have a criminal background or a violent past.

Regardless of what they tell you, it is your responsibility as a woman to shield yourself from any blowback or hardships that you could potentially inherit due to a relationship you have with someone.

Unfortunately, there are conniving and deceitful men out there, and you need to do your due diligence by legally confirming that yours is not one of those deceivers. This type of information is well worth paying for! Knowing what you're getting into up front will not break the bank. Do your homework to know the type of man you're getting serious with before you get really serious.

Gemstone, spending $60 to $100 today can save you from spending $60,000 to $100,000 (or more) later, not to mention the heartache and pain you might wind up with after making a serious commitment to someone unworthy...like saying "I do."

DECEMBER 9 GEM
Trademark yourself.

Gemstone, think of the top three words that describe who you are.

Are you young, successful, and powerful? Strategic, closer, and trendsetter? Fabulous and fun with impeccable style? Creator, visionary, and shrewd? Timeless, graceful, and top-tier? Foxy and fearless with fresh perspectives?

Yes, you yourself are a work of art, an invention, a masterful creation, a whole intellectual property that needs to be legally registered by giving yourself your own stamp of approval.

Trademark yourself.

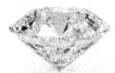

DECEMBER 10 GEM
Before jumping the broom.

Gemstone, it's critical that you and your soon-to-be spouse both get physicals 60 to 90 days before "sealing the deal" in marriage.

Knowing the status of each other's health is imperative *before jumping the broom* and "becoming one."

Are you both healthy people? Are there any underlying health issues that need to be discussed? Does this person have HIV, STDs, or any other diseases that could affect the marriage?

The physical health of both individuals will affect the marriage, so be sure to add this very important step to your wedding planning checklist!

DECEMBER 11 GEM
Details matter.

Stop surfing for CliffsNotes and get into the details!

- ✓ Details help you understand things better.
- ✓ Details communicate that you care.
- ✓ Details keep others engaged.
- ✓ Details are part of the strategy.
- ✓ Details win games.
- ✓ Details earn degrees.
- ✓ Details impart patience.
- ✓ Details speak to being able to fully complete projects without having to repeat any parts of the process.
- ✓ Details create proficiency.
- ✓ Details foster safety.
- ✓ Details solve problems.

Details most certainly matter—so, get into the details, Gemstone!

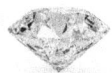

DECEMBER 12 GEM
What are you willing to tolerate?

Gemstone, to get to the next level in life, you may have to endure a few unpleasurable things.

You can't always get around having a bad professor or a terrible boss unless you quit...which can cause major setbacks in accomplishing your goals.

If there's a clear and definite end to what you're tolerating—such as the class will end in a few months or the boss will soon retire—then it may be worth sticking things out. However, make a list of what you're willing and not *willing to tolerate.*

Stick to your toleration limits to avoid your boundaries being crossed or your beliefs and values being disrespected.

DECEMBER 13 GEM
Haters.

Say hello to your *haters* and welcome them to hate you! Why? Your *haters* are your biggest motivators.

These evil-eyeing, sour-sucking, yip-yappers are exactly what you need to keep you going. They are the ones who constantly remind you of what they think you're incapable of achieving.

Gemstone, you only have one job, and that is to prove them wrong. Do so quietly. Retaliate by ignoring their antics and skipping merrily along as you pursue your goals.

Talk about a slow burn and good feel once you achieve your goals right in front of their faces! The hate they spewed will have been well worth it, because that will have given you the push you needed to get there.

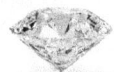

DECEMBER 14 GEM
Play stupid games, win stupid prizes.

Gemstone, engaging in illegal, illicit, and/or unethical behavior will absolutely get you hemmed up.

Therefore, be fully ready to receive the consequences of the irresponsible things you do, because while maybe you'll be forgiven once or twice for playing stupid games, after three or four times, you'll be done.

Stop now while you still have some sense! Don't be a winner of stupid prizes—those prizes are never favorable.

DECEMBER 15 GEM

The batteries in your back.

Is someone controlling you? No one should have that kind of power over you!

You're a grown woman with your own mind—you are not a controlled or roweled-up Muppet.

Don't allow others to convince you to do something or go in a direction you don't want to go in! Don't do their dirty work or their bidding or be their "ish starter." Gemstone, you are too smart for that! You can think for yourself.

Unzip the skin on your back and yank out the Duracell, Energizer, or off-brand batteries that someone else put there. Use your own intelligence and common sense—and the guidance of a mentor or respected person—to make sound life decisions.

DECEMBER 16 GEM
Three plans.

Strategic people always plan for the best and are prepared for the worse.

Have three plans:

- ✓ Plan A: This is your primary plan and assumes that all things will fall perfectly into place.
- ✓ Plan B: This is the back-up plan you put in place in case Plan A falls through. It maintains some of the elements of Plan A but has a few tweaks.
- ✓ Plan C: This is the plan you go with when you completely have to abort your original and back-up plans and take a whole different route.

Gemstone, having *three plans* in place means that you are not planning to fail.

DECEMBER 17 GEM
Past and future.

To have a future, a past must exist.

The feelings of pain, hurt, suffering, toxicity, and regret may be connected to your past and you may wish for them to stay there, but without your past Gemstone, you would not have a future.

Your past designs what you want your future to look like.

If you didn't get to travel as a child but wanted to, then your future may focus on traveling the world. If you were an only child growing up and always wanted siblings, then you may want to marry and build a large family of your own. If you were deceived as a teenage girl, then your future may be connected to becoming a motivational speaker or author who can teach young girls how to avoid traps and deceptive people.

Reflect on your past and see how the things you might be ashamed of or even deplore can actually be impetuses for the amazing future you'll then embark upon.

DECEMBER 18 GEM
It's giving nothing.

If someone or something is not "feeding" you by helping you develop personally, professionally, intellectually, or spiritually, then the relationship *is giving nothing.*

Surround yourself with people who feed you and vice versa, because if you're not being fed, you are malnourished, and if you're malnourished, you're dying.

And what do we say to the God of Death, Gemstone?

"Not today!"
—Arya Stark, *Game of Thrones*

DECEMBER 19 GEM
Be unapologetic and unselfish.

Many astute women today find themselves having to diminish their brilliance to make others feel comfortable for their lack thereof, but you need to be intelligently *unapologetic and unselfish.*

Dummying down your intelligence to appease others is not an option—it goes against every reason to be intelligent.

Your elite ingeniousness is their problem and never yours; it is never the problem of the one who possesses it.

Gemstone, never apologize for your intellect! Rather, be generous with it. Share your wisdom and teach other inquisitive minds what you know so that they can "know what they don't know."

DECEMBER 20 GEM
Pay the cost.

Gemstone, if you want to be the boss, you must *pay the cost.*

What's the price?

Putting in hard work, handling employee and customer complaints, bearing the full responsibility of your team in terms of them meeting organizational goals, handling workplace drama and insubordinate employees with grace, finding the best talent, ferreting out sick leave abuse, correcting poor personal initiative, managing workplace politics and excessive meetings, setting the direction over and over again, dealing with employee unions, terminating employees, steering displacements, getting 360° feedback, dealing with bad supervisors, sitting in all-day leadership trainings, admitting mistakes, seeking buy-in from your team, having to overexplain tough decisions, managing no-shows and employee strikes, putting in late work nights, working during your vacation time, writing reviews, and receiving bad management surveys from employees.

That's quite a high price.

Are you sure it's worth the expense? Be sure to count the cost before becoming the boss.

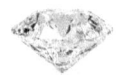

DECEMBER 21 GEM
Leave it for tomorrow.

Gemstone, if there's something you absolutely cannot finish today, put it down and pick it back up tomorrow.

Don't beat yourself up about not getting it done. But do allocate enough time tomorrow to tackle it, because many people find the start of a new day to be quite forgiving.

DECEMBER 22 GEM
Say their name.

When someone has inflicted pain on you, it's a strong indication that you've finally overcome that pain when the hurt no longer resurfaces when you say or hear their name.

This happens because "time heals all wounds," as the saying goes. Time gives space for elevation and maturity to occur, both of which invite forgiveness and forgetfulness into your heart. Or you may just no longer care about the person who hurt you.

Gemstone, when you can *say their name* and the misery, pain, and hate no longer exist, you are no longer powerless—you have set yourself free!

DECEMBER 23 GEM
Jealous people attack first.

It's easy to point out jealous people—directly or in a roundabout manner, *they always attack first* by saying what they envy the most about you.

Their insults may be direct or subtle, but even when they're subtle, oftentimes you'll pick up on what they're really saying because you'll sense or feel their negative energy.

Gemstone, know that whatever they use to attack with first is usually what they most envy about you.

DECEMBER 24 GEM
Healing wounds.

According to the National Library of Medicine, "Oxygen is vital for *healing wounds.*"

Gemstone, likewise, your emotional hurts and pains need oxygen.

"Air out" your emotional wounds by talking about the source of your pain in confidence with your therapist or someone else you trust, because oxygen—that purest element of airflow—is essential for repairing what's damaged you.

In order for this to work, no one can want the heavy heart-healing you need more than you, so work through what you need to work through by airing it out. Only then can you move forward in life.

Do the real work that you need to do to heal whatever has emotionally wounded you.

DECEMBER 25 GEM
The truest words.

The *truest words* are the hardest to hear.

As they say, Gemstone, "the truth cuts like a knife." But how can you properly digest your steak without it first being cut up?

The truth must be told no matter how it's sliced or diced.

DECEMBER 26 GEM
By your life span.

The woman who lives to be 101 would be considered quite young at the age of 21—perhaps she's even an adolescent then. The girl who lives to age 24 would be considered fairly old at the age of 19. The woman who lives to age 93 would be middle-aged when she's 47.

This is very telling about how age should really be viewed, which is *by your life span* and not your current chronological age. Therefore, the plan is to live a long, healthy, and prosperous life.

Gemstone, no matter your age, the goal is to make each day count (refer to the July 15 Gem). Today can either be the peak of your life or the beginning of it! Choose the latter of the two.

The beautiful thing about *your life span* is that you have a lot of say-so when it comes to the length of it because of how many things you can control. You can confess to wanting—and pray to have—a long life and you can choose to take care of yourself.

If you control the way you live your life, you can control your age and you can live well and live long.

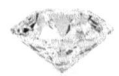

DECEMBER 27 GEM
Monkey bars.

Letting go of things in life that you need to let go of can be so hard!

It's not always easy to just move forward and quickly transition to a new way of doing things, such as ending a relationship that needs to end, leaving a career you love for the sake of pursuing your passion, decreasing the time you spend with friends you adore to focus on your soul, or pressing forward after the loss of someone close to you.

But like when you were once a child playing on the *monkey bars*, to move forward, you must let go of the bar you're hanging onto so that you can grab the next one.

Let go of the *monkey bar* you're holding onto right now and grab the next one in order to further advance towards your purpose. Gemstone, it's the only way.

DECEMBER 28 GEM
A real gentleman.

"Chivalry is not dead."

In fact, Gemstone, chivalry should be "alive and well" in your book, and you need to let him know that if he seems to have forgotten.

A real gentleman:

- ✓ Opens your door.
- ✓ Allows you to go first.
- ✓ Compliments you.
- ✓ Is courteous to you, your family, your friends, and others.
- ✓ Is respectful.
- ✓ Is polite.
- ✓ Is fair in conversation.
- ✓ Tips well.
- ✓ Acknowledges you in every room that he invites you.
- ✓ Shares with you.
- ✓ Exhibits patience while courting you.
- ✓ Puts you at ease.

If he cannot consistently demonstrate having a solid 80% or more of these qualities, then inform him of what is expected of him, because these expectations need to be nonnegotiables for you within the relationship.

DECEMBER 29 GEM
Let sleeping dogs lie.

If the argument that occurred last night really didn't bother you or the other person involved, then leave it there come morning.

Gemstone, avoid instigating trouble with others when it's not worth it! As the saying goes, *let sleeping dogs lie.*

If going from dusk to dawn has caused the disagreement to blow over, then let the disagreement stay blown away in the wind.

The point is to pick and choose your battles.

Leave senseless things to rest—especially when they've already been forgotten—and move on with life.

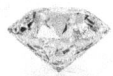

DECEMBER 30 GEM
Simply unique.

Refrain from comparing yourself to other women, because every single woman on planet Earth is different.

Your intricate details make you *you.*

You have different skills, desires, and dreams than other women do; you have a different upbringing and background than other women do; and you are beautifully shaped in your own special way.

Another woman's journey is not your journey—your experiences in life are customized just for you.

Your life's puzzle pieces are designed with different shapes, cuts, and sizes, and the more puzzle pieces you have, the more of a masterpiece you are.

You, Gemstone, are *simply unique.*

DECEMBER 31 GEM
Kick her!

When you see potential in another woman but she needs some help seeing it for herself, *kick her!*

That little kick—given through words of encouragement, support, direction, and guidance—may be the very motivation she needs. Stay on her; check on her.

Be your sister's keeper.

Gemstone, when one woman wins, it's a reminder that all women can win.

NOTES

JANUARY 27 GEM

The Matrix. Film. USA: Warner Bros., Village Roadshow Pictures, Groucho Film Partnership, Silver Pictures, 3 Arts Entertainment, 1999.

FEBRUARY 3 GEM

Winfrey, Oprah. "Oprah Explains How Your Life Whispers to You—All the Time." *Oprah Daily*, August 10, 2021. https://www.oprahdaily.com/life/a37055443/oprah-listening-to-whispers/.

FEBRUARY 6 GEM

Daquis, Sophie. "Malama Life." YouTube. YouTube, December 30, 2017. https://www.youtube.com/channel/UCDn5zbDIhRG97O2rqia9Gag.

MARCH 9 GEM

Doane, Corey. "11 Science-Backed Benefits of Smiling [Infographic]." The Mindfulness Meditation Institute, February 18, 2021.https://mindfulness-meditationinstitute.org/2021/02/18/11-science-backed-benefits-of-smiling/.

MARCH 25 GEM

Kaufman, Josh. "The First 20 Hours—How to Learn Anything." TEDxCSU. YouTube, 2013. https://youtu.be/5MgBikgcWnY.

MARCH 28 GEM

Inspector, Dr. Yoram. "The Surprising Way Emotions Can Affect Your Gut Health." Netdoctor, October 13, 2018. https://www.netdoctor.co.uk/healthy-living/wellbeing/a27361/the-surprising-way-your-emotions-can-affect-your-gut/.

MAY 25 GEM

Greenberg, Melanie. "The 3 Most Common Causes of Insecurity and How to Beat Them." *Psychology Today*. Sussex Publishers, December 26, 2015. https://

www.psychologytoday.com/us/blog/the-mindful-self-express/201512/the-3-most-common-causes-insecurity-and-how-beat-them.

JUNE 3 GEM

Richo, David. "13 Strategies to Deal with Your Emotional Triggers." *Experience Life*, September 30, 2020. https://experiencelife.lifetime.life/article/13-strategies-to-deal-with-your-emotional-triggers/.

JUNE 9 GEM

López, Isbelia Esther Farías. "What Is Superwoman Syndrome?" Step to Health, March 16, 2020. https://steptohealth.com/what-is-superwoman-syndrome/.

JUNE 17 GEM

Smith, Jennifer. "31 Simple Ways to Free Your Mind Immediately." Lifehack, February 9, 2021. https://www.lifehack.org/articles/communication/30-ways-free-your-mind-immediately.html.

JUNE 21 GEM

Andrews, Dr. Shawn. "Why Women Don't Always Support Other Women." *Forbes*, December 10, 2021. https://www.forbes.com/sites/forbescoachescouncil/2020/01/21/why-women-dont-always-support-other-women/?sh=4706a0443b05.

JUNE 30 GEM

Goewey, Don Joseph. "85 Percent of What We Worry About Never Happens." *HuffPost*, December 7, 2017. https://www.huffpost.com/entry/85-of-what-we-worry-about_b_8028368.

JULY 7 GEM

Robbins, Mel. *The High 5 Habit: Take Control of Your Life with One Simple Habit*. Carlsbad, CA: Hay House, Inc., 2021.

AUGUST 8 GEM

The Tinder Swindler. United Kingdom: Netflix, 2022. https://www.netflix.com/title/81254340.

SEPTEMBER 18 GEM

Badaracco, Joseph L. "Defining Moments: A Framework for Moral Decisions." Boston: Harvard Business School Publishing Class Lecture, 2003. Electronic. (Faculty Lecture: HBSP Product Number 2861C.)

OCTOBER 1 GEM

Munroe, Dr. Myles. "10 Keys To Maximizing Time," YouTube. Munroe Global, 2022. https://www.youtube.com/watch?v=kwt9fSj8OYo.

OCTOBER 4 GEM

"Fertility Gamechanger? New Study Confirms Female Eggs Choose Their Sperm." NZ Herald, September 22, 2020. https://www.nzherald.co.nz/lifestyle/fertility-gamechanger-new-study-confirms-female-eggs-choose-their-sperm/MTYMDAY2WFZS3NVE6UQIVFB5CA/.

OCTOBER 6 GEM

Chapman, Gary D. *The 5 Love Languages: The Secret to Love That Lasts.* Chicago: Northfield Publishing, 2015.

NOVEMBER 21 GEM

"Talk That Talk" (Audio) Ft. JAY Z. YouTube. The Island Def Jam Music Group, 2011. https://youtu.be/Z8FarCnm1mE.

DECEMBER 6 GEM

Chunn, Louise. "The Psychology of the to-Do List—Why Your Brain Loves Ordered Tasks." *The Guardian*, May 10, 2017. https://www.theguardian.com/lifeandstyle/2017/may/10/the-psychology-of-the-to-do-list-why-your-brain-loves-ordered-tasks.

DECEMBER 24 GEM

Castilla, Diego M, Zhao-Jun Liu, and Omaida C Velazquez. "Oxygen: Implications for Wound Healing." Advances in wound care. Mary Ann Liebert, Inc., December 2012. https://www.ncbi.nlm.nih.gov/pmc/articles/PMC3625368/.

www.ingramcontent.com/pod-product-compliance
Lightning Source LLC
Chambersburg PA
CBHW060854120626
46553CB00001B/80